TIME MANAGEMENT
FOR TEACHERS

Essential Tips & Techniques
BY SCOTT PURDY

Also by Scott Purdy

Tomorrow Begins at 3:00
Teaching Students to Write - Grades 3-9
The Write Time Teacher Planbook
A Hands On Approach to Teaching Statistics, Probability, and Graphing
A Hands On Approach to Teaching Measurement
A Hands On Approach to Teaching Logic
A Hands On Approach to Teaching Geometry
A Hands On Approach to Teaching Algebra
A Hands On Approach to Teaching Patterns and Functions
A Hands On Approach to Teaching Number and Operations

For information, please contact

WRITE TIME PUBLISHING
2121 Rebild Drive   Solvang, California 93463-2217
(800) 824-3376
FAX: (805) 688-7802
e-mail: howt@silcom.com

Contents

Introduction

Twenty-four hours per day. That's all we get. Into this twenty-four hour time period, we have to compress our time at work, time for our families, time for hobbies, time for sleep, and time for ourselves. How we organize and choose to use these hours is our decision. It all becomes a matter of priorities.

Unfortunately, priorities are often rearranged or forgotten due to *obligations*. The culprit is usually our work. Regardless of how much you enjoy teaching, it's a job that can become all-encompassing, even obsessive in terms of filling your twenty-four hours.

With the six hours per day you spend in the classroom, the time spent preparing, grading, talking to parents, meeting individually with students, going to meetings, taking classes for units, thinking about your students who have problems, driving to work, and falling asleep at 8:30 because you can no longer keep your eyes open, life can become a blur.

Even your weekends can become filled with school. Too tired to do much of anything on Friday night, catching up with grading on Saturday, and planning or collecting materials on Sunday are all too common occurrences for many teachers. Basically, if there are spare moments, teaching obligations can fill them.

I remember operating this way for the first few years that I taught in inner city Los Angeles. But little by little, I began to discover approaches I could use to lessen or eliminate some of the time I was spending on teaching. These were small changes such as writing a test in a certain way to make it easier to correct, assigning jobs to students to keep the room clean, delegating many of the classroom procedures to students, and having parents help with preparation of materials.

By making these adjustments, I began to find some time to pursue other interests. After school I taught guitar, eventually giving as many as sixty half-hour lessons per week. With this "extra" money, my wife and I were able to buy property in Colorado. Over several summer vacations, while living in a tent, we built a house (by ourselves) and in 1980 moved with our two children to Ouray, Colorado.

I got a teaching job and soon after school started, the superintendent asked if I'd be interested in administration. In Los Angeles, administration was of no appeal but in a small town in Colorado, why not give it a try? I ended up taking fifty-six units in eighteen months, while teaching full-time. I also found time to build and sell a second house, and we had our third child during these years.

In 1986, after six years as a teacher, principal and superintendent of schools in Ouray, we moved to Solvang, California. For the past thirteen years I have been a teacher, principal, and superintendent of a K-8 school with 700 children.

In 1987, seven of my fellow teachers and I formed a publishing company (Hands on, Incorporated) and we have since written and published seven math books.

At Solvang School I've been fortunate to work with outstanding and dedicated teachers. Working together, we have managed to pass a local bond issue and build new classrooms and

2

a 10,000 square foot gymnasium. We've been recognized as a California Distinguished School. We've been able to set up two computer labs, institute an early primary education program, and initiate a myriad of other unique programs.

In these "Solvang" years with my wife and family, we've done two additions to our house, have become the shipping department for Hands On, Inc., have watched our daughters graduate from college (one of whom has carried on the family tradition and is currently teaching fifth grade), and our son begin his college career. Over these past few years, I've written this book along with two others -- one teaching students how to write more effectively and a second book on time management.

I mention all of this with the purpose of convincing you that you can accomplish anything you set your mind to if you are *organized, establish priorities* and *adhere to your priorities.*

I'm very proud of what I have accomplished, but I could not have done any of this if I had not learned to manage my twenty-four hours each day.

In June of 1995, I stepped down from administration and returned full-time to the classroom because there were too many things I still wanted to accomplish. *Teaching has given me the free time I needed to accomplish these goals. Time management for teachers can work for you, too.*

Time...to Begin

As teachers, we have accepted a huge responsibility -- the education, nurturing, safety, and welfare of young people. Parents trust us, for six hours per day, with their children. There is no greater responsibility.

Along with this tremendous obligation, teaching is hard work. It is frustrating, disillusioning, exhausting, hazardous and demanding. Studies show that the average teacher works fifty-four hours per week. What is unusual about our work is that these fifty-four hours allow no extended lunches away from work, no special fringe benefits, and no closing the office early to celebrate the birthday of a co-worker.

Our schedules are highly structured, not unlike the assembly line worker who must stop and start at the whistle. But in our case, we're not assembling inanimate parts, we're working with enthusiastic, vulnerable, impressionable children. We are truly *in the trenches* all day.

I wrote this book with two purposes in mind: first, to provide practical ways to gain control of your teaching time; second, to provide a different *slant* on how we view ourselves as professional teachers.

I don't believe that teaching needs to be a fifty-four hour per week job. Thirty-five hours per week seems reasonable since we are actually in the classroom, with students, for only twenty-eight hours per week. To this end, I have tried to present techniques which will allow a substantial reduction in time spent "doing our job."

I also feel that society should view us far differently than it does. In order to achieve the status we deserve, we're going to have to change the way we treat ourselves and the way we present ourselves to the public at large. To generate this change, we need to show everyone with whom we come in contact that...

...teachers are *Professionals*
...teachers are *Managers*
...teachers are *Unique*

Teachers are Professionals

Professional: "*a person who has advanced and specialized training in liberal arts or science and applies this training in mental rather than manual work; including such professions as medicine, law, teaching, and engineering.*"

This definition should clearly define our role. Teaching is not just "another job." We have a scientific body of knowledge which is specific to our occupation. We make life-changing decisions day in and day out. We continually must retrain and upgrade our methods to reflect the changes in our specialties. Yet, for some reason, society doesn't generally acknowledge our status, and worse, neither do we! We don't view ourselves as being anything more than... teachers. This must change!

Physicians, attorneys, dentists, architects, investment bankers, and other professionals who deal with the public seem to have an "air of arrogance" about them. While this sounds derogatory, it's not meant to be. They exude a sense of self-respect that the public generally accepts and admires. They believe they're special, they dress like they're special, they conduct professional offices and yes, they can make money like they're special.

And what do teachers do? We sometimes dress in jeans, sweatsuits, and shorts; we have unkempt classrooms; we allow people to seek our opinion (conference) without appointments; we argue over petty issues, forgetting about things that are important; we allow parents to debate or intimidate us on issues in which they have no background or understanding. In short, we are often our own worst enemies.

This doesn't mean we don't do a good job of teaching! It means, we aren't doing a good job of representing our profession to the public. Maybe it's because there are so many of us or maybe it's because everyone *went* to school so *everyone* feels that he or she is an expert on education.

Whatever the reason, we must assume our role and be professional in every sense of the word. You certainly won't convince all of your fellow teachers to change, but you can change your own point of view and in so doing, earn the respect you deserve.

Teachers are Managers

Manager: "A person who has charge of or directs, conducts, and administers others in a supervisory and motivational role."

7

As a teacher, you are the chief executive officer, chairman of the board, and president of your own corporation of thirty employees. Your classroom is corporate headquarters and your product is the education of your students.

You are in charge of more people, in a more volatile environment, with more supervisors (parents and administration), than 95% of the managers in the world! This link to business is unmistakable. Approach your job as a business manager and the critics outside of school will begin to understand that you face the same problems and dilemmas that they face in their world. Your classroom is your business. Let parents and students know that you know how to run your business and that your business is successful!

Teachers are Unique

Unique: "One and only; different from all others; having no like or equal."

One of the greatest things about teaching is that it allows almost complete freedom in the way you operate your classroom. School rules and obligations aside, when the door is closed, you are your own boss, and you can be as unique as you want to be. Very few occupations allow this amount of creativity and freedom.

In the context of this chapter, when I say teachers are *unique* I'm referring to the fact that we are different than other professionals in regard to our outlook on life. We became teachers knowing that our pay would never be equivalent to a corporate attorney or a surgeon. We chose this profession because we have an extra dose of humanism and patience. For some reason, we want to give something to our students and by

8

giving, we get something intangible in return. It can't really be described but it's there.

We should all take pride in our ability to care about and help others. We have *"no like or equal."*

The ideas presented in this book pose many opportunites to sharpen your professional, managerial, and unique skills. Effectively managing your time will make you a more organized, more thorough, happier, and better teacher. It will also give you some time to start working on your dreams.

●　　　●　　　●

Before you begin reading the chapters that follow, a few more points to remember...

First, there is very little discussion of instructional methods or delivery of curriculum in this book. Consultants abound who will suggest ways in which to change or improve your delivery of information to students.

This book accepts that your teaching style is unique and comfortable to you. My purpose is to give you some new ways to think about the mundane tasks of teaching -- grading papers, preparing for a substitute, classroom management and discipline, and dealing with parents.

Second, for many teachers, preparing for lessons, grading papers, thinking of new lessons, and collecting materials is a hobby. If you love what you do and want to spend your free time working on school projects, I salute you! However, I think you will still find ideas that you can pull from these pages that will simplify some of the professional tasks which perhaps you don't enjoy completing.

Third, throughout this book you will be presented with many new and different ways of looking at your work as a teacher. There are ideas which you will be able to use immediately and others which you will need to adapt or adjust to your particular circumstances. Some you'll simply reject. Not all of the ideas apply to everyone.

Fourth, while I certainly don't claim to "know it all," this book is an attempt to share "all that I know" about managing your time as a teacher.

Making the Grade

Grades, what an incredible mystique they hold. They unleash the praise or wrath of parents, they are the source of acceptance or rejection from college, and they provide a means of peer comparison of children throughout the world.

Yet as powerful as grades are, most teachers question what they represent and generally dislike the process of generating them in the first place. Yet, we do what we must do. Grades are an inherent drawback of the profession.

If, however, you are spending excessive amounts of time correcting papers and recording grades, you are taking time away from planning, meeting with students and parents, and from other personal pursuits. There are some different approaches you can try which will shorten the time commitment you make to grading papers.

There are three reasons for correcting papers. We need to see student work to adequately evaluate progress, students need to have corrected work returned so they can analyze and improve their performance, and we need grades to "justify" our marks on report cards (administrative requirements may drive you crazy, but leave your idealism behind for a bit and accept the realities of teaching).

Based upon the "reasons" for correcting, you must establish *what* and *how much* correcting you will do.

You must first determine how many grades you need to justify a report card mark. How many minutes of your time each day you are going to allow for correcting papers? How much time each weekend? How often will you need to provide input to your students as to how they are doing? How much do your students value receiving feedback in the form of a grade? How soon are you going to get their papers back to them?

Teachers work from so many different settings with so many varied constraints that it is impossible to offer universal conclusions. But, here's a starting point from which to proceed.

How many grades do you need to justify a report card grade?

Many teachers who are reading this have a grade book nearby with meticulously kept daily grades for each of their students. You are probably reading this book because you're tired of the time it has taken to create this listing of grades. Other readers may have very few grades in their grade books, have a stack of papers to be corrected (which were left at school) and are wondering how they can keep up to date on grading and still have time for other activities.

A "standard" which you might be able to live with is one grade per week in each subject area. This seems sufficient, justifiable, and reasonable. Based upon this approach, you will have nine grades per quarter (eighteen per semester) to average; definitely a sufficient number to reflect the student's performance throughout the school term.

Primary teachers are in the unique situation of not giving letter grades to students. Primary report cards usually consist of a different type of grade structure (checks or "pluses," etc.). Nevertheless, you still must demonstrate to parents that these marks are based upon something more than the way you *feel* about their child's progress. In terms of meeting face to face with parents, it behooves you to have a system which supports your report card symbols. You need to show a weekly progress mark for each of your students.

For middle and upper elementary teachers, one grade per week per subject is relatively easy for spelling, reading and math. It's more difficult in social studies, science, and physical education. You will need to plan -- in advance -- your method of grading in these subjects.

If you teach in a departmentalized setting, you may need to restructure your grading procedures. As a teacher of senior English for several years, I had difficulty keeping my correcting to one grade per week; eventually, I accepted one writing grade and one test (in some form) per week as my standard.

In my current situation, teaching eighth grade writing, I find that one grade per week works well. Typically, students have a grade for an extended essay of some kind every two weeks and on alternate weeks have a packet of vocabulary work or perhaps a monthly test grade. (I don't give a lot of tests.)

The important point is that you must set your level of what is sufficient for your situation. Once you have made this decision, you have a plan to which you can adhere and begin to implement.

This does not mean that you don't have other information about student performance in your grade book. Homework assignments, daily activities, class participation, bonus points, and extra credit are all part of the grading procedure (portfolio assessment and alternative assessment become an additional component to traditional grading and filing), but these should be handled as *in class* correction as described later in this chapter. In terms of actual grades, *reduce your correcting to one grade per subject per week.*

How many minutes of correcting are you going to do each day? Each weekend?

Four hours of correcting per week is a maximum for most teachers. This breaks down to roughly thirty minutes per day. Junior and senior high school English teachers may have to add several hours per week due to the necessity of having children write extended papers.

Don't assume that getting to thirty minutes of correcting per day is easy. It takes planning and organization, but it establishes a time frame which is reasonable. Once you've set the time frame, you do planning which allows you to adhere to this constraint.

You will also need to decide how many papers and what type of papers you will collect and correct -- homework, classwork, tests, projects, etc. One grade per week per subject area will narrow this decision for you.

As a writing teacher, I correct seven hours above and beyond my time in the classroom each week. That works out to be one hour per day, seven days per week. On the other hand, I have much less preparation than many teachers. My assignments are ongoing -- for at least one week -- so my prep time is kept to a minimum. Every teacher's situation is unique. The key factor here is to set a time frame that establishes when "enough is enough." My personal goal of seven hours per week includes all grading and preparation.

How often do children need to receive teacher input?

Students need teacher input every day, but grades are not necessarily the input they need. One minute (or less) spent face to face with a student discussing what has been done correctly and then constructively showing what can be improved is far more beneficial than returning a paper with a grade and teacher comments.

This doesn't mean that students don't need to receive grades, it means that grades are a secondary issue. Correcting papers for two hours each night to provide "input" is of minimal value.

Students need to hear from you every day. They need to know you care and that you know what they are doing. They also need to know that you will not accept less than their working to a maximum capability. A grade does not satisfy any of these needs. A one minute conference does.

How much value do your children place in receiving feedback in the form of a grade?

Quite a lot, but undoubtedly for the wrong reasons. Grades are the measuring method of parents, test scores are the measuring method of administrators and the media. Children are generally more concerned with receiving the teacher's approval and recognition (college bound high school students excepted). The grades are merely a language that they understand.

We need to give students feedback which they value and from which they will learn. Red marks and a grade are not necessarily the key to accomplishing this. If you accept this, it puts the time you spend correcting into a different perspective.

How soon do students need input?

All of us like instant feedback but it is not always possible to get papers back to students immediately. We often face extenuating circumstances as do our students.

There are several ways to accomplish a short turn-around time, but our goal must be never collect a second set of papers until the first set has been returned. For self-contained teachers, this means within each subject area. For example, don't collect a second math paper until the first has been returned, etc.

You may ask how this is possible, but realistically, unless a paper is returned to the student before he completes another assignment, there is probably no need to correct it in the first place.

Formatting for speed

If you want to speed up the process of correcting and begin implementing some of ideas presented thus far (how many grades, how long each day, how often and how quickly) you need to establish a *Plan First, Correct Next* system. It's so simple and so obvious, yet so rarely done. Formatting for speed is one component of this system.

Have you ever gone through a set of papers in record time and wondered how they seemingly corrected themselves? They were probably formatted efficiently.

Planning or organizing a paper for quick correcting takes time but provides a return of "two for ten;" that is, two minutes spent now saves ten in the future. A well-planned class set of thirty papers can easily be corrected in fifteen minutes; the same paper, poorly planned, can take forty-five minutes or more.

Look at the examples on pages 18 and 19. These are samples of a test designed for fifth grade American History. They are typical of tests which a publisher might provide or which a teacher might create. The samples are shortened to fit on one page to make comparison easier. They basically contain objective questions, but the ideas presented on the next few pages can relate to essay questions as well.

Sample A will work, Sample B is formatted for speed.

Look at the multiple choice format in A. Students are asked to circle the correct answer. In sample B, they write the letter in the blank space. Have you ever seen how some students circle answers? To correct test A you would need to scan across the entire page thirty times, in Test B all answers are in a line.

Most teachers avoid creating matching tests because they are hard to set up and only test lower level thinking skills. In terms of testing for a lot of factual information in a "quick to correct" format, matching questions are the best. The trick is to set up answers so they create a real or nonsense word. The phrase can be top-down, bottom-up, middle out, etc. By the way, the answers for sample B are: B-E-D-F-L-A-C-K.

Setting up the matching format in sample A is a bit faster, but trying to follow students' lines from column A to B is impossible. The answer column does not need to use A, B, C, etc. Any letters will do.

You could use BEDFLACK or you could create a phrase in which the first letter of each word is the correct response. For example, the answers could be: My Sister Irene And Her Brother Rudy Eat Popsicles Every Wednesday Night. When you create the test, use the letters M, S, I, A, H, B, R, E, P, E, W, N.

Yes, there are two E's. Your E response would say:

E. Answer not given

American History Test - Age of Exploration

I. Circle the correct answer

1. The Norse colony in Greenland died out because
   - A. Many people from Greenland moved to Vinland.
   - B. Norwegian leaders stopped sending supplies.
   - C. The Indians and colonists were fighting.
2. De Soto explored the south...
   - A. before Magellan began his voyage.
   - B. after England started colonies.
   - C. before Quebec was founded as a colony.
3. Who were the first Europeans to start a colony in America?
   - A. the Spanish
   - B. the Chinese
   - C. the Norse

II. Draw a line from the explorer to his discovery

A. Cortez
1. Explorer who claimed the southeast   B. de Soto
   for Spain   C. Coronado
2. An African who looked for golden cities   D. Fray Marcos
3. The Spaniard who "saw cities of gold"   E. Estavan
4. Fray Marcos' Indian friend   F. Zuni
5. America was named for this explorer
6. Explorer who claimed Mexico for Spain   G. Aztecs
7. The southwest explorer who was Spanish   H. Pueblo
8. A Spaniard captured by the Indians   I. Columbus
                                              J. Magellan
                                              K. Cabeza de Vaca
                                              L. Vespucci

III. Fill in each blank with a short answer

1. Christopher Columbus tried to find someone who would pay for his trip across the _____ ocean.
2. European sea captains searched for trade routes to the _____.
3. _____ was a busy seaport on the Mediterranean Sea.
4. Astrolabes and _____ measured how far north of the equator ships sailed.

IV. On the attached paper, write a short answer to each question.

1. What was Columbus's purpose in his voyage and why was his approach different than other sailors of his day?
2. What areas did the Spanish explore and what was the purpose in exploring these areas?
3. What was the "northwest passage" and who searched for this passage?

18

Sample Test B
American History Test - Age of Exploration

I. Write the letter of each correct answer on the blank line

_____ 1. The Norse colony in Greenland died out because
          A. Many people from Greenland moved to Vinland.
          B. Norwegian leaders stopped sending supplies.
          C. The Indians and colonists were fighting.

_____ 2. De Soto explored the south...
          A. before Magellan began his voyage.
          B. after England started colonies.
          C. before Quebec was founded as a colony.

_____ 3. Who were the first Europeans to start a colony in America?
          A. the Spanish
          B. the Chinese
          C. the Norse

II. Write the matching letter in the blank space

                                   A. Cortez
_____ 1. Explorer who claimed the southeast   B. de Soto
        for Spain   C. Coronado
_____ 2. An African who looked for golden cities   D. Fray Marcos
_____ 3. The Spaniard who "saw cities of gold"   E. Estavan
_____ 4. Fray Marcos' Indian friend   F. Zuni
_____ 5. America was named for this explorer   G. Aztecs
_____ 6. Explorer who claimed Mexico for Spain   H. Pueblo
_____ 7. The southwest explorer who was Spanish   I. Columbus
_____ 8. A Spaniard captured by the Indians   J. Magellan
                                     K. Cabeza de Vaca
                                     L Vespucci

III. Write the correct word for each --(?)-- in the blank space.

_____ 1. Christopher Columbus tried to find someone who would
        pay for his trip across the --(?)-- ocean.
_____ 2. European sea captains searched for trade routes to the--(?)--.
_____ 3. --(?)-- was a busy seaport on the Mediterranean Sea.
_____ 4. Astrolabes and --(?)-- measured how far north of the
        equator ships sailed.

IV. Write a short answer to each question.

1. What was Columbus's purpose in his voyage and why was his
approach different than other sailors of his day? _____

_____

2. What areas did the Spanish explore and what was the purpose in
exploring these areas? _____

_____

3. What was the "northwest passage" and who searched for this passage?

_____

19

You can correct a set of thirty papers in two minutes if you set up your matching questions as described. The *fill in the blank* section in sample B is much faster to correct since all answers are once again in a line.

To correct the first three sections of this test, you can lay the papers out as shown. Since all of the responses are in a left

hand column, you can correct several papers at the same time plus have the benefit of comparing answers to see if several students missed the same question. Perhaps that indicates that something is wrong with the answer key or that there are two or three possible responses for the same question.

Definition, explanation, and short answer questions take much longer to correct, so you might consider limiting your use of this type of question. Three to five is reasonable and seven or eight is a maximum. Any more than that and you will spend too much time correcting. Remember, *plan first, correct next.*

You should always plan tests with writing space on the test sheet rather than having students use their own paper. When you add a second sheet of paper to a test you begin to slow down the correcting process.

The ideal test uses the front side only. If you have more to ask, use $8\frac{1}{2}$ by 14 inch paper, reduce the size of the font, or use a xerox machine to shrink the page to a smaller format. If you still have too much to test, create two versions, duplicate on different color paper, and alternate test forms as you distribute them to students. You can then complete other tasks while students are testing (they can't copy with different test forms), and you will only have half as much to correct as you would if all students were asked all of the questions. I will guarantee that students will provide the same grade distribution if the test is only one half as long.

On the sample test, due to lack of space, the short answer questions probably have too little room for a response. Typically, these questions would "spill" over to the back of the test sheet. It is always better to use the back of a sheet rather than a second piece of paper.

The sample test did not include any extended essay questions. Essays take a long time to correct and although they probably the best indicator of student understanding, they need to be used sparingly. To me, tests which consist of five essay questions seem sadistic, not to the student but to the teacher who must correct them. It takes a lot of time to read and correct one paragraph or essay. To face 150 responses on a test (five questions times thirty students) is too much to ask of your time!

If you have a variety of essay questions you would like to use, discuss the questions in class and ask students to respond verbally. A second approach would be to work together as a class to write one "perfect" response to the essay question. This becomes a class activity with all students gaining understanding, and there is no after-class correction to be done. Another approach would be to list five questions and have each student respond to one question. In short, avoid numerous essay questions on tests.

If you use "pre-fab" tests as provided by book publishers, do a cut and paste process to make your correcting easier. Paste in answer blanks or create your own answer sheet. Design test that the average student can complete in twenty minutes. If you give longer tests, many students won't finish in the allotted time, and you will spend your lunch time or recess monitoring those students with incomplete tests. In the scheme of your teaching, the tests are not that important!

Formatting for speed can be done in areas other than tests. On all homework and classwork papers you assign, be a stickler for structure and organization. There is nothing wrong with the traditional approach of using an answer column in math or having students fold their papers three or four times to create boxes in which to do various exercises.

Kindergarteners through high school seniors can fold their papers in one way or another to speed up your correcting. Folding is much more effective than having students draw lines. Often when you ask students to do something as simple as, "draw a line down the center of the paper," the result looks like an experiment in divergent thinking. Folding works better.

When assigning papers in which students write sentences, have them skip a line between each sentence or better yet, write sentences one through ten on the front of the paper and eleven through twenty on the reverse. You should also have them pre-number their papers before they start writing.

Folding and numbering activities are valuable educational experiences as they involve listening, following directions, and organizing. By having students fold and number their papers, you have created "standardized" format for correcting. All papers can be turned over at the same time, every "problem number 11" is in the same location, and work which is incomplete is very easy to identify. Every paper which you collect and every homework assignment should be formatted. You will be amazed at the time you will save.

Correcting Without Collecting

Eighty percent of work which students do should never be collected. This is a second part of the Plan First, Correct Next system. Correcting without collecting doesn't mean you don't see their papers, and it doesn't mean papers aren't corrected. You merely correct them without physically collecting them and in most cases you don't worry about recording a grade.

There are a variety of ways to do this, all of which you have probably used before but maybe not to the extent necessary to be really effective.

You can have students exchange papers, form cooperative groups to discuss each student's paper, display student work on an overhead or opaque projector so the whole class can provide input, have students correct their own papers, circulate the classroom and correct papers while they're on the students' desks, have two or three class members act as "correctors" for a given assignment, or decide not to correct an assignment.

When students correct their own papers or have a classmate correct them, there often is a concern expressed about "cheating." True, some students may change answers in midstream, or perhaps be accepting of an "e" that looks very much like an "i" in a spelling word. Realistically, doesn't it make more sense to have the student correct the mistake rather than have the teacher mark it wrong?

When you correct daily work and hand it back, you have an idea of what the student doesn't know, but the student hasn't gained any practice in identifying or correcting his or her mistakes. Research indicates that it takes a minimum of six to seven presentations of information for most students to gain mastery. Why not let the student correct his own paper the first five times, and you correct it when there's a *chance* at mastery?

When a student changes an answer on a worksheet or homework assignment, attribute it to the learning process. Encourage them to change answers; encourage them to work together to find solutions. If you decide to record a grade for that assignment, there's nothing wrong with every child getting an A or a "plus." In future work and on tests there will be ample opportunity to validate their performance and understanding. Returning a set of papers with each error circled, only to watch half of the class throw them away without even looking, seems like a terrible waste of the time you spent correcting.

If you question whether a student understands a concept, call on him or her to verbalize the answer. Give help if the student seems confused and let him or her rewrite or reconstruct the answer. Taking this time in class is much more time efficient than your taking a paper home, giving a low grade, and returning the paper the next day.

To give another example of *correcting without collecting*, imagine a fourth grade lesson dealing with two place multiplication. If students have already been exposed to the process and are practicing, you can use different approaches. You might hand out a set of ten to fifteen problems, explain the first two or three to the group, have students complete the worksheet, collect the papers and correct them at home. This is traditional and will take five minutes of your directed time in class and twenty minutes of your free time at home.

On the other hand, you can follow the same procedure but when students have worked for fifteen minutes or so, read answers aloud letting student correct their own and have them work in teams to finish. Explain that the only papers you will record in your grade book are those which have all of the correct answers.

Given another fifteen minutes, eighty percent or more of your students will have a "plus" or 100 (whatever system you use for daily work) in the grade book (record grades as students finish). Those without grades are students who need extra help. You have now spent thirty-five minutes of classtime, have no papers to take home and you already know with whom to work individually the following day.

An alternative would be to collect all papers, return those which are all correct, and keep the papers of those students who are having problems. Spend ten minutes reviewing the problems and plan your next day accordingly. With this approach you'll be looking at five papers instead of thirty.

An approach to use throughout the day, in any subject area, is rather than giving students the class period to work independently, *spend your entire time teaching*. With each worksheet problem or sentence, vary the way in which you present it. For example, on number one, explain it yourself as you write it on the board; on number two call a student forward to write the example; number three, call up several class members to do the work simultaneously; item four, have different students do different parts of the task; item five, have one student explain the process from his seat while another student does the writing in the front; etc. While all of these different approaches are going on, each student is "copying" the explanation on his or her own paper. You will find that the questions asked using this approach are far more focused than if you have students work individually.

The benefits of this approach are many. Discipline problems are lessened as students generally enjoy listening to one another. When you have completed the lesson, every paper is finished and is done correctly, and there's nothing to collect or correct. You have eliminated the need to circulate the room, answering the same questions over and over again; students are getting directed learning throughout the class period; and you are getting an idea of how individual students can perform the task.

This approach is both time and learning efficient. Remember that you must vary the approach as each problem or task is done. If you try to use the same method of explanation time after time, students will turn off and will begin working independently.

For a teacher, assigning a page in a workbook or worksheet and giving students time to complete it in class is easy. When you assign extended (more than ten minutes) work for students to do at their desks while you attend to other tasks, you are creating a grading workload. Restructure your teaching so that assignments are done as described previously or are in short (five minute) activities which which are corrected immediately. This five minute cycle of work-correct-work-correct will keep your students on task and your after school responsibilities to an absolute minimum.

The step-by-step teaching for a full class period is far more demanding of you during the school hours, but once the school day has ended, you will have almost nothing to correct. In addition, your students will probably have a better understanding of the lesson.

If you use this approach you will be amazed at the time you will free up during your after school hours.

A final point regarding this approach. You need to *collect* and *correct* papers at some point in time. But through your planning, you will collect only enough papers that can be corrected in the time frame you've set for correcting. Always *plan first, correct next.*

Avoid deferred teaching

The last few paragraphs have introduced this idea, and it is the third aspect in the *Plan First, Correct Next* plan. It means that while you are in the classroom, direct the lessons as much as possible. We have all had days that we were unprepared, unmotivated, or were not feeling well. Just getting through the day is a challenge.

The tendency in these situations is to assign work for the children to do. You know the scenario: "Open up your books to chapter two and read the first section. When you are finished answer the the questions on page 45 and 46. Be certain you answer in complete sentences."

For forty-five minutes, the students work dutifully while you recoup. Unfortunately, at the end of the time period, you have a stack of papers which are unformatted and unstructured. You have deferred teaching to your after school hours.

The best thing you can possibly do on days you're not feeling well or are not fully prepared is to direct the lessons all day. Do class discussion activities, read chapters aloud as a class, read a play aloud as a class, read a book to the class, and answer all questions orally. If you need a break from this, have students read silently in a "free reading" book for fifteen minutes here and there throughout the day. But don't assign busy work that you will have to correct later.

Your goal should be to get through the day with nothing to correct. Spend your time after school preparing for the next day so when you leave school, you can "leave school."

Collecting and Returning Papers

This is as much a classroom management issue as a grading concern, but since it is tied to grading, I'll discuss it in this chapter.

How do your students turn their work in when it is complete? Do you collect their papers in a certain order? Are they stacked randomly in a paper tray? Do you ask one student to collect papers? Most teachers use a variety of techniques but if you want to speed up the process of grading and recording grades, try some of the these ideas.

For homework or daily assignments (you shouldn't be collecting these, by the way), don't have students pass them in or place them in a container as they are completed. Either have a separate cubby hole (mailbox) for each student or have them keep their papers until you are ready to collect all of them.

Call students' names in reverse grade book order to bring them up to you. As a student comes forward, it gives you time to quickly peruse the paper, give brief praise for work that looks neat and complete, notate and refuse a paper with is incomplete, check for a name, and mark in your grade book which students have completed the assignment. All of these tasks can be completed in three minutes by having students bring papers to you. You'll either spend your time in class or spend your time after school or at home.

By collecting papers in reverse grade book order, recording grades is simple with no searching for names up and down the list of student names. When you get into this routine, you can return *yesterday's* set of papers as each student brings *today's* paper up to you. Everything is in order!

Another benefit of this approach is that when a student tries to hand in unfinished work, you recognize it right away and don't accept it. If you simply collect the papers in a bin, students have usually disappeared for the day before you notice that an assignment is incomplete, which means two more days of handing the paper back and forth.

It may sound as if calling each student's name to bring his or her paper forward will take a lot of time away from instruction. On the contrary, you can use this time to keep a running dialogue going with the class. You can stop every now and then to read a paper aloud, do a "mini" lesson when you notice that several student have made a similar error, ask each student a pertinent question as they are walking to the front, or you can praise individual students immediately for the work they're handing in. It's a very powerful, individualized, and time efficient technique.

A second approach to collecting and distributing papers is the use of "cubbies" or student mail boxes. Each student has his or her own cubby hole (similar to a teacher's lounge mailbox), and all papers are handed in and returned through this cubby. Once again, papers can be collected in grade book order and handed out the same way.

The benefits are that less time is spent in the process of handing work in and students can turn work in immediately upon completion. Ongoing or day-long assignments can be handed in after the "collection" time without disrupting the "order" of the papers and students (especially younger students) like having their own mailbox.

The drawbacks are that you don't know until the end of the day (or class period) if students have completed the assignment, you don't have the attention of the class focused on individuals for praise, and feedback to students is not instantaneous. Nevertheless, it's a time saver and a good method of organization.

Many teachers use a system in which each student has his or her own file folder. When a student finishes work, it is placed in the folder. While this keeps papers organized and in a order, I find it somewhat cumbersome to go through thirty folders and pull out each student's papers. It also adds something more to carry to your car if you decide to take the folders home and do correcting there.

It is, however, another approach to consider.

Other approaches to correcting efficiently

There are a number of specific ideas you can use to speed up the grading process. In this section, twelve ideas are presented. Some will work for you, some you may reject, but it's probably worth giving each of them a try at some point.

The most powerful workforce in your classroom is students. In terms of correcting, they provide a ratio of 1:1 so it makes sense to use them.

When your students do expository writing, have them proof and correct (or even grade) one another's papers. They need guidance and guidelines to do this effectively. You can use a form similar to the one on the next page to have them focus on specific elements.

I have used a chart similar to this for correcting student essays for many years. I use my computer to print this information on 1" by 4" mail labels and affix the label directly onto the student's paper. This saves shuffling an extra piece of paper.

Name_____

Corrected by: _____

_____ Punctuation (10)
_____ Spelling (10)
_____ Usage (10)
_____ Opening Paragraph (20)
_____ Body Paragraphs (10)
_____ Closing Paragraph (20)
_____ Overall Effectiveness (10)
_____ Neatness (10)
_____ TOTAL

This is a simple format that can be changed to use in almost any grade level (except early primary). Simply staple this form to the essay and have students exchange and grade papers. You might give them a chance to do a rewrite, based upon peer input, before you collect the final copy. Another application would be for each student to correct his or her own paper using this correction form.

⊕ Another way to speed up the correction of essays and longer written assignments is the "three mistake rule." Many students are quite careless about errors in writing mechanics. They write the last word of an essay, rip it from the notebook, and hand it in -- without proofing.

To heighten students' awareness of the importance of proofreading, you might begin reading only as far as the third (or fifth) mistake you find. This includes spelling, punctuation, grammar and usage. As soon as you have circled or identified the third mistake, stop reading and return the paper to the student to be rewritten.

When it has been rewritten, once again, read to the third mistake and return it to the student for rewriting. There will be occasions when students will have to rewrite papers five or six times, but you will also find that within a matter of weeks or months, students start having their friends or parents help them with their editing.

The outcome is that eventually you get papers with few errors (other than structural errors which you meet with the students to discuss). Students quickly get the message that proofreading is essential from their own time management perspective.

A drawback to the *three mistake process* is the record keeping in handing papers back and forth. On the other hand, if you are reading through a student's paper and take the time to identify twenty or thirty mistakes, you are accepting a burden that should be the responsibility of the student. Remember, you are not the student's editor.

🕐 Most schools have overhead projectors available to teachers. If your copying machine can make transparencies, duplicate three or four of your students' writings onto transparencies. These should be good papers to use as models. Display them one by one on the overhead and have the class discuss what makes them effective.

The students who did the work are receiving recognition for excellence and students who need improvement are seeing models for future work. It's part of the "two for ten" principle. Two minutes spent showing the desired outcome, saves you ten minutes in correcting work that has "missed the mark."

🕐   A tried and true method which is used less and less in the classroom is having students write answers, sentences, responses, etc. on the whiteboard or chalkboard. It's visual, it's efficient and children love writing with markers or chalk. It may seem passé but it is a great way to correct without collecting.

🕐   You may experiment with having children use only the front side of papers you will be correcting. Often, correction becomes confusing because you have to turn papers over at different times since children number differently or because their handwriting is of different sizes.

     It isn't hard to stay to the front side if you plan shorter assignments or format papers for students as described previously. If this seems wasteful, use both sides but put a different subject area or different assignment on each side of the paper.

🕐   Emphasize neatness on every paper completed by students, regardless of the subject area. Neatness on the part of your students will save countless hours of your time. You might even offer bonus points or awards for students who do particularly neat work.

     If we stress neatness for the students, we have to accept neatness as our standard as well. At times, many of us are guilty of distributing papers which are messy or have been sabotaged by the duplicating machine. We have to model our expectations, and that includes our handwriting on the chalkboard or whiteboard. Take the time to write neatly.

     The quality of work generated by each individual varies widely, but incorporating a neatness grade as one of your standards will save time.

⏱   A great time saver is the idea of "selective correcting." If students have done a number of similar math problems, spelling sentences, or answered a given set of questions, you can select only certain items to correct (i.e. problems 3, 7, 13, and 19). By looking at a small sample you will be able to tell which students understand the concept or assignment.

If the information is such that you want to be certain that students get correct answers for each question (perhaps in content areas) you can hand papers back and go over the answers of non-selective items as a class.

A rebuttal to students or parents who complain that you have not corrected every response is that, "The piano teacher isn't there every time you practice." Every note played and every word written need not be heard or viewed by the teacher. Individual practice, drill, and repetition is part of the learning process.

⏱   If you just can't seem to eliminate the number of papers you are correcting, consider hiring someone to do the repetitive correction work. Assignments such as those with objective questions, math problems, sentences with spelling or vocabulary words, etc. do not necessarily take teaching know-how to correct. These mundane papers can be corrected by anyone other than yourself.

Your son or daughter, a neighbor, a retired person, or a former student can do much of your correcting and recording of grades. You can offer to pay them on an hourly basis or arrange a "per set" price. Hiring someone for one or two hours per week at seven or eight dollars per hour is money well spent if you feel bogged down by correcting.

Arrange with this person to *correct by exception*. This means that all papers done satisfactorily can be recorded and returned without the teacher even looking at them; all papers which indicate non-understanding by a student should be given to you for your perusal (have the person use a paper clip to "flag" incorrect papers).

When you consider the hourly amount you make as a teacher, it is probably worth fifteen dollars per week to have someone do some of your work for you.

☺ If your teaching assignment requires students to write long papers, essays, or reports on a consistent basis (English teachers, for example), you might consider offering extra credit for early submission of papers.

This contradicts some of the correcting and collecting ideas presented earlier but it can lessen the impact of receiving thirty papers (150 papers for a high school English teacher) on the same day.

On a one hundred point grading system, offer students the option that any paper handed in prior to the due date will receive a five point bonus. If ten percent of your students hand them in early, you can spread the correcting over several days. Although you'll still be faced with a sea of papers to correct, having fifteen papers corrected and back when the remainder of students hand in their assignments can help your outlook.

Other benefits include: sample essays to use as models while other students are still working on their papers, and eliminating other extra credit work by offering this option as the only means of gaining extra credit in your class.

☺ For the next several days, time yourself when you correct papers. Use a stopwatch or timer and see how long it takes you to correct individual papers. If you have a set of thirty papers and each takes five minutes to correct, you'll spend two and one-half hours completing the task.

There's not much you can do about the papers in your hands but you may plan differently when you realize that correcting takes this long. You may find that after you time yourself, many ideas in this chapter become more appealing.

An interesting correcting idea which can save time (depending upon how organized you are) is the use of a cassette tapes to correct papers.

Have each of your students bring a cassette from home. On assignments such as term papers and reports you can save yourself a lot of writing by recording your comments as you read the paper. A taped discussion might sound like...

"Mike, I'm looking at your paper and the presentation is very nice. The title is centered on the page and your topic, 'All Abuzz about Beekeeping,' is very clever. As I turn the page and read your opening paragraph (pause to read) I'm looking for a thesis statement as well as your method for creating interest in the opening sentence. I assume your thesis is the third sentence (read aloud), and it's good although you might have added something like (record your suggestion)."

Continue your dialogue as you read through the paper. Continually talking to Mike as though he were at your desk and you were talking face to face.

After using this method, many teachers find that it becomes an indispensible tool for providing a great amount of individual feedback and actually takes less time than correcting by traditional means. Students really enjoy listening to the tapes as do their parents. One caveat here -- be absolutely certain that you make one positive comment for every criticism!

The only drawback is collecting and keeping track of the tapes. It can get confusing to store tapes and papers so you might use a manila envelope for each student, or you can purchase a cassette tape carrying case. Some cases will hold as many as sixty cassettes, and if you label slots in the case with student names, you can tell who has and who has not returned tapes to you.

I discovered many years ago that trying to track the back and forth movement of one tape per student was very time consuming. I now simply keep a bin of tapes and cross out the name of the previous user and write the next student's name. Every once in a while, there is a minute or two of conversation at the end of the new recording, but since I never say anything very negative, I've never had any student make any more than just a passing comment. I found it doesn't matter.

⊙ When you have a stack of papers to correct and you just can't bear to sit down with the entire pile, correct one or two each time you plan on leaving the room. Leave the stack on top of your desk and before you go to the teacher's lounge for coffee, correct two; before you take your recess break, correct two; while students are doing silent reading, correct two; etc.

This technique also works well at home, especially over the weekend. Keep the stack of papers accessible and each time you walk by, correct two.

You probably won't get the entire set corrected in this way, but you'll find that instead of having thirty papers to correct, you'll have already graded ten or twelve by the time you sit down to do the rest. It's an effective way to make a molehill out of a mountain.

Consider using the *Plan First*, *Correct Next* approach to help you with your planning and correcting.

For the next two or three weeks when you finish your teaching day, look at the number of papers you have to correct, set them aside, and plan the activities for the following day. Do your duplicating, worksheets, gathering of materials, etc. before you correct anything. If you have a stack of papers that will take three hours to correct, plan so that you collect nothing the following day; if you have very little to correct, plan to collect one or two sets of papers that will fit into your correcting time frame.

It takes time to develop a new habit. If you'll stick with this plan for three weeks you'll save yourself hours of time, feel more positive about teaching, feel much more relaxed during your off-school time, and you will make it a habit to *plan first, correct next.*

Disciplining
Your Management

Self-discipline, organization, and efficiency are words which define the essence of this chapter. Time efficient people are organized. They don't plan every moment nor do they lack spontaneity. It's simply that their day-to-day lives have a structure that allows them to complete all they must do and still have time for relaxation and entertainment. Organization does not constrict, it liberates.

If you "scramble" each morning trying to get youself, your family, and your household organized; if you walk into your classroom and face a mess from the day before; if your students leave your room at 3:00 with the classroom in disarray; or if you never seem to have a spare moment, you need to discipline your management at school and at home as it pertains to school.

Seven areas for possible improvement include:
1. Plan the night before
2. Write everything down
3. Put your work force, your students, to work for you
4. Revamp your classroom and your supplies
5. Establish procedures for student activities
6. Develop a plan to handle absentees and new students
7. Plan more efficiently using a two for one return

Every work morning, when you arise, you have a remarkable array of tasks to complete and decisions to make. You must decide what to wear, what to eat, what to complete before school starts, what to put in your kids' lunches, what you'll have for lunch, what you need this afternoon at the market and the list goes on. If you wait for the morning to get yourself organized, you will start every day stressed and from then on spend most of your time coping with the day rather than living it.

If you will take fifteen minutes the night before *and* allow yourself ten extra minutes in the morning, you'll find that each day will be more enjoyable and that you will be in charge of your time.

Before you go to sleep each night...

● Lay out your clothes and know what you are going to wear. If you need to press or wash or something, do it in the evening or choose something else to wear.

● Write a list of *everything* you need to do the next day. Organize and plan your day around accomplishing these obligations. Plan time to relax and have fun.

● Take a minute or two to think ahead to the next few days and write down how you might combine some of tomorrow's tasks to accomplish future obligations as well. For example, if it is Monday night and you have several parent conferences on Thursday afternoon and evening, decide what you will wear, what your family will need in your absence, and try to organize for Thursday as you complete Tuesday's trip to the market, to day care and the dry cleaner.

● Think about how long each task will take. A list of twenty obligations may look insurmountable, but you might be surprised how quickly things can be accomplished once they are on an all-inclusive list.

● If you crave coffee first thing in the morning, get it ready the night before so it is ready at the flip of a switch. If breakfast is a hassle, set the table and get the toaster and cereal out the night before. If you make lunches for the kids, either have them make them or be certain you know what you're going to make.

● Set the standard for your children (and spouse) to be organized. They'll wear you out or wear you down if you don't work on this together. This includes lunch money, homework, parent notes to be signed, after school activities for the following day, and transportation to school.

● Put your glasses, your keys, your purse or briefcase, and your school paraphernalia by the door. Eliminate the last minute morning search.

These few preparations take minimal amounts of time but make the "morning after" a much more positive start for your day.

Write *everything* down

If you don't have an organizer of some type, you must begin using one. It needn't be elaborate or expensive, but it should have one page per day to allow you to write down everything you need to remember -- in one place. It should be small enough to carry with you at all times. If you use a lesson plan book, it can double as your organizer. It makes sense to keep *everything* you need to do in one place. This includes writing all daily or weekly school bulletin information in your organizer.

Writing things down becomes a habit. If you depend on your memory, you may wake up in the middle of the night only to recall obligations you've forgotten. If you write *everything* down, once you've made your nightly list of "to do's," you can be assured that your list is all inclusive and you can forget about it until morning.

You might also consider writing down your requests of others as well. If you need the custodian, your principal, a fellow teacher, or a student to carry out some activity, a written note is far more reliable than a verbal message. Carry a few 3" by 5" cards with you for this purpose.

Along with writing things down in your organizer, you need to write things for your students. One of the most efficient ways to help organize your students is by using charts. Whether you are graphing how many teeth each child has lost, their performance on learning multiplication, how many candy bars they've sold in the latest fund raiser, or what assignments have been turned in and which are missing, posting these for students to see is very effective.

Making charts can take a long time but thanks to the magic of the the Xerox machine, you can now take an eight and one-half by eleven inch sheet of paper to your local "instant printer" and for three dollars they will make a 36 by 48 inch poster (several smaller sizes are available as well) which you can use for charting student activities.

Many departmentalized teachers wouldn't have even considered making six charts (one for each class period) for display in the room in the past, but now you need only type or print out a list of each class on graph paper, take it to the printer, and they will duplicate the charts you need. This makes writing it down for students very simple.

Put your students to work for you

Your greatest allies in being organized and in control at school are your students. Generally, there are twenty-five to thirty-five eager to please individuals just waiting for your direction (some exceptions apply). They should become your cleaning crew, bulletin board designers, librarians, sorters and filers, and messengers to their homes. If you've not organized this work force, get them on board as soon as possible.

If you are totally pleased with the custodial crew at your school, you are an exception. For some reason, custodians and teachers are like oil and water. What you want cleaned, they don't see and what they clean, you don't notice. It seems that unless we watch the cleaning take place, we're often not convinced that any cleaning was done.

If you want to have a clean (and organized) classroom, you should depend upon the custodian as little as possible. Your goal should be to have your classroom sparkling clean every time your children leave the room, at recess, at lunch, at the end of each class period, and at the end of the day.

It takes a small amount of organizing, but two minutes of time by each student at the close of each period translates into an hour of cleaning by one person.

Identify the tasks that need to be done to keep your room neat. A list might include: chalkboard, white boards, book cabinets (back and front), wastebaskets, floors (in three sections), desktops (in three sections), supply table, sink, countertop at sink, bulletin boards, AV equipment, chalktrays, erasers, stapler and pencil sharpener, and alternates or "subs."

Three minutes before the close of each class period or session, give students two minutes to do their jobs. The job chart can be written on chart paper (railroad board). Cut small slits to hold cards with students' names, or use clothespins with students' names written on them. Students have one job for two to four weeks and then jobs are rotated (names are moved).

White boards	Darcy	Desks 1	Kimmy
Chalk boards	Travis	Desks 2	Martin
Bookcase - back	Amy	Desks 3	Jake
Bookcase - front	Anna	Supply table	Marcus
Wastebaskets	Micah	Sink	Brett
Floor 1	Siobhan	Chalktrays	Doug
Floor 2	Nicki	Eraser	Jred
Floor 3	Carlos	Sharpener	Sonya

After two minutes of cleaning -- set a timer to ring -- quickly scan the room to be certain everything is in place. If a job is not complete or is poorly done, that student receives no "bonus" point. Every student who has cleaned properly receives a point. These points are computed into their work habits grades. The process is quite simple since generally, every student receives a point each day or each session. Don't even enter them in the grade book, simply make a note of the negative points, that is, those students who have not satisfactorily completed their tasks.

This approach can be used with students from first graders to seniors in high school. It is very effective. It keeps the classroom in excellent order, teaches students that they too have a responsibility to keep things clean, and it eliminates almost all dependence upon the custodians.

Do you spend a lot of time and money in preparing bulletin boards for your classroom? Those efforts and expenditures should stop, today. Those are not your bulletin boards, they are the students' bulletin boards, and *they* should design and make them. You may provide guidelines and materials if you choose, but the students should be doing the work. If students design the boards and maintain them, then they will look at them and learn from them.

You can organize a student bulletin board project in a variety of ways. In a self-contained classroom, with numerous boards to be decorated, put students in groups and have them work together to plan their boards. If you don't want to use class time, have students work in pairs or trios and design boards as a homework project. If you teach a departmentalized schedule, have students prepare bulletin boards as part of ongoing projects, class competitions, or bonus point/extra credit opportunities.

If you teach very young children, begin a cross-aged tutoring program with a fellow teacher who works with older students and have them design and assemble your bulletin boards.

Having students design and create bulletin boards is not shirking your responsibility as the teacher. It involves the students in creating their classroom environment. It *should* be a student activity.

If you are spending *any* of your time sorting, filing papers, or collating sets of papers, you're taking another responsibility away from students. They should know and understand your filing system and they need to be aware how long it takes to put thirty packets of information or projects together. Let them collate, let them staple, let them fold, cut and paste. Put the silver platter away and get them involved in their own education. It does take time away from lesson delivery but these are tasks that teach responsibility, teamwork, cooperation, listening, organization, neatness, and understanding. It is time well spent.

If you have a library in your classroom or if you take your class to the library, students should be trained to do checkout, check-in and refiling of books. Sure, they will make mistakes, and it will take time to train them, yet they can and should do this for you. They should also be held completely accountable for keeping your *in class* library neat and organized. There is nothing magical about straightening, sorting, or filing books. If students can alphabetize, they can take charge of your library.

Perhaps the most important role your students can assume is their daily grapevine to parents. You can save yourself phone calls and hours of misunderstandings by requiring that students always take notes home to parents and bring them back signed the following day. Make this standard operating procedure regardless of the age of your students. When a note goes home from the PTA, the principal, or from you, three hole punch the note or have students place it in a specific place in their backpack or folder and give a bonus points or a reward when you see the signature the next morning. These points are added into their work habits grade.

You will be surprised how most parents appreciate your efforts. The students may complain about it, but your communication with parents becomes continuous and consistent. If a student habitually forgets to bring notes back, it's time to call home. In the interim, you'll save many calls and many complaints such as, "I have no idea what is going on at school" or "The teacher never tells us anything."

Never underestimate the ability or desire of your students to take responsibility for work which we teachers feel obligated to complete. It is their (the students') education and they must accept that their role is more than learning the "three R's."

Organize your classroom and supplies

Budgets, vandalism, safety, theft, storage, and furniture make this aspect of organization unique to each teacher. What you *should* have, what you *do* have, and what you *can* have may well comprise three lists with very little overlap. Yet without basic supplies it's very difficult to operate an organized classroom.

The challenge is to have everything you need close at hand with as little out of pocket expenditure as possible. A reasonable list of supplies (depending upon grade level) includes:

staplers and staples	a pencil sharpener	paper punch
pens/pencils	paper clips	rubber bands
teacher scissors	scissors for each student	markers
chart paper	locking file cabinet	dustpan
colored pencils	flash cards	post-it notes
chalk/erasers	crayons	construction
paper	glue/glue sticks	index cards
rulers	overhead projector	paper towels
broom	spray cleaner	sponges
newspaper	old magazines	kleenex
projector screen	tape recorder(s)	wall maps

A second aspect of organization supplies is assuring that you can find things that you have stored. *You should be able to put your hands on any item in your classroom within one minute.* Many teachers are hoarders by nature, but if you have so much stuff that you can never seem to find what you are looking for, or if you have closets full of boxes that are all labeled *miscellaneous*, begin organizing your materials.

The goal of a good filing or storage system is to make it generic enough that you will never again enter your room with any materials without immediately knowing where they should go. The boxes are for three dimensional items, your file folders are for paper and thin magazines.

One of the best ways to do this is to buy several packages of stackable storage boxes. Some afternoon or Saturday, lay out ten (twenty if you are a primary teacher) of these empty storage boxes in your room. You needn't label them yet, you can figure out your system as you go. Open one of your storage closets and begin sorting your treasures. There are many ways to organize: by months of the school year, by subject, alphabetically, etc. You will probably have some false starts and do some rearranging as you come up with your system, but force yourself to put your supplies in boxes.

Try to throw out twenty-five percent of the stuff you have stored. If you haven't used it for three school years, you will probably never use it again. Get rid of it. Label each box clearly and stack them so you can see what you have. If there is no location in your classroom in which you can put the boxes for storage, use peel and stick shelf paper to cover one end of the boxes and line them up against one of your walls. A stack of boxes neatly labeled can look impressive.

Depending upon how long you have been teaching, this can take anywhere from a few hours to many days, but when you've finished you've taken a big step in organizing your classroom.

Your desk is another very important feature of your overall efficiency in your room. Develop a filing system for your file drawer which allows you to keep papers out of sight and organized. There are entire books written on developing your personal file system, but in my experience I suggest you adhere to three basic ideas.

First, label your file folders in "generic" terms. Don't create a file folder for every paper. If you have folders that say things as specific as , "Staff Meeting, Jan. 24," "Staff Meeting, Jan. 31," "Staff meeting, February 6," your principal may think you are a hero, but you are wasting your time, not to mention file cabinet space. If you have file folders with titles such as, "Where the Red Fern Grows, Chapter 1, First Activity," "Where the Red Fern Grows, Chapter 1, Second Activity," etc. you need to simplify. On the other hand, if your file systems has titles such as, "Stuff for spring," "Ideas from college," and "math worksheets," you might want to buy a few more folders and become a bit more focused.

Second, use color coding and give the colors a meaning in your mind. I recommend that you put everything you will file in sixty-four folders -- eight folders of eight different colors. With this variety to choose from, you need to organize all of your subjects and topics into eight categories. Years ago, as a self contained teacher, I used the colors red, blue, green, yellow, orange, maroon, purple, and grey. You may cringe at my system and if so, create your own. But devise something that makes sense to you.

Red reminds me of "read" so I put my language arts materials in red folders. Maroon is a dull color so I put administrative obligations, policy, bulletins, and beauracratic information in these files. Green reminds me of science. Yellow reminds me of music so I use this for extra curricular areas. Orange has no meaning whatsoever to me, but I use it for history and social sciences. Blue is my favorite color, and I use it for my professional files. Purple is my literature color. Gray reminds me of the color of pencil lead so I use this for math. Of course, this system is foolish, but sometimes it's easier to remember things that are silly than things which make sense.

Third, within each color group limit yourself to eight subgroups. This makes filing and retrieving very simple. Be as generic as possible

RED - Lang. Arts	ORANGE - Social St.	GREEN - Science	BLUE - Professional
1. Assignment sheets	1. Unit 1	1. Life Science	1. Credential paperwork
2. Projects/centers	2. Unit 2	2. Earth Science	2. Sub masters
3. Homework packets	3. Unit 3	3. Physical Science	3. Labels
4. Book Reports	4. Unit 4	4. Science Projects	4. Keepsakes
5. Punctuation	5. Unit 5	5. Films/Resources	5. Equipment info
6. Spelling-Usage	6. Unit 6	6. Posters/overheads	6. Classes to take
7. Vocabulary	7. Sample projects	7. Generic assignments	7. Summer school
8. Creative writing	8. Maps	8. Reports/occupations	8. Open house/B to S night

PURPLE - Literature	YELLOW - Extra Curr.	GRAY - Math	MAROON - Adm.
1. Literature book 1	1. Music/Dance	1. Basic Operations	1. Bulletins/Policy
2. Literature book 2	2. PE	2. Geometry	2. Parents/Support groups
3. Literature book 3	3. Health	3. Measurement	3. Grades/Report cards
4. Literature book 4	4. Art	4. Fractions	4. Meetings/Committees
5. Short story unit	5. Computer	5. Decimals/Percent	5. Special Ed/ESL
6. Poetry unit	6. Holidays	6. Games/Activities	6. Requisitions
7. Plays/extra reading	7. After school programs	7. Puzzles/enrichment	7. Testing
8. Word games/fun	8. Performance ideas	8. Misc. ideas	8. September

If you keep your subgroups simple yet distinct, you will be able to access and file papers quickly. Files which you use less often should be kept in a filing cabinet while papers you access often should be kept in your desk file drawer. The color coding should be consistent between the various locations of files.

If you have resource books and catalogues lining your room, put them in boxes, file them, recycle them, or throw them away. Remember that after one year the prices and offerings have changed. There is no point in keeping old catalogues.

Oversized paper and posters are difficult to store. Art supply stores have a wide variety of artist portfolios which are great for storage. They come in many sizes and are large enough to fit almost any poster you might purchase. Smaller portfolios made of clear vinyl make good storage containers for construction paper and scraps of paper. Buy one portfolio for each color of construction paper and you'll find your messy cupboards will be clean and organized. You will also have much less waste.

If you supply scissors, crayons, glue, colored pencils, erasers, and other art supplies for your students, organize them in closable containers which stack (these can also be used for math manipulatives and calculators). You have a choice of spending a lot of money on *designer* containers at *storage* boutiques *or* you can go to a restaurant supply house or discount warehouse and buy stacks of one hundred styrofoam containers (used to box hamburgers) for three or four dollars. Store the containers in one of the stackable cartons used for milk delivery and you'll find that organizing your materials can be done very cheaply.

Write a student's name on each container and make them responsible for the inventory of their supplies each time the container is used. If you teach in a departmentalized setting, write numbers on each container and give students a corresponding number during each class period. It may take some time to organize the containers at the beginning of the school year, but when you want use them, distribution and accountability is very simple.

Establish procedures for everyday tasks

An important part of daily classroom activities involves mundane tasks such as students entering and leaving the room, attendance, dismissal at the end of the day, distributing play equipment, bathroom use during class time, drinks of water, sharpening pencils, distributing or collecting papers, "loaning" pencils or pens, moving to the front of the room for rug activities (for younger children), and setting up and cleaning up art projects.

There are many ways that these procedures can be handled. Several are mentioned in various sections of this book as they pertain to other classroom activities. Some examples of unique procedures you might implement include...

When a student asks to borrow a pen or pencil, ask for collateral -- a watch, set of keys, or some other personal item which he or she values. One teacher I know bought boxes of the short pencils golfers use. When students come unprepared, she gives them a golf pencil. Students aren't too fond of these and end up bringing their own more frequently.

Offer some type of ticket system to students which can be redeemed for "no homework nights." Give each student a certain number of tickets per week/month, and if they need to leave the classroom to get water or a book from a locker, make them give up a ticket. There is not penalty in this system, simply a reward for those students who take care of their personal needs at the appropriate time.

For students who request a week's work while on independent study, duplicate a set of appropriate activities with spaces for you to check off specific requirements. When a student misses class for a week, there is no way this work can ever be "made up." Many parents don't seem to understand this. I find that a special independent study sheet acts as a bit of a deterrent for parents who capriciously pull their children from school.

The procedures you establish for these daily/weekly/ monthly recurring events can either simplify or complicate your life. Keep experimenting in each area until you find a procedure that works. If you are being interrupted by kids sharpening pencils, leaving the room for a drink of water or a locker trip, spending half an hour preparing an independent study, or using ten minutes of class time to distribute papers to students, begin establishing set procedures. Teaching is hard enough without losing your train of though every few minutes with a non-essential interruption.

Develop a plan for absentees and new enrollees

One of the greatest frustrations in teaching is monitoring students who are absent. Regardless of how well organized or how thoroughly planned you may be, chronic absentees and poor class-wide attendance can drive a teacher crazy. Consider this three-step approach to help in coping with this situation.

First, begin from day one emphasizing to students and parents the importance of being in school every day. Write about it in newsletters, discuss it in class, and offer rewards or bonus points for monthly and weekly perfect attendance by individual students and for daily perfect attendance by the entire class. If you have one less absence per day by conducting this campaign, it is time well spent.

Second, identify one student each week to act as the "absentee" secretary. The secretary should collect a set of all papers distributed each day for each absent student and write their names on the papers; a simple form can be completed by this person (often called a "We Missed You") which identifies the events/lessons of the day. The "We Missed You" form and sets of student papers are given to the student upon his return.

Third, don't make being absent easy. Regardless of the reason for an absence, the child who is not in school has missed between four and six hours of instruction. This time is gone, never to return. If a student returns to class and completes three worksheets in fifteen minutes and that is the total amount of work required to complete for the missed day, that student might be inclined to be absent again.

While you don't want to punish a child for begin sick, you do want to assure that the child thinks twice about missing school for "feeling a *little* sick," buying a new pair of shoes or a prom dress, or babysitting a younger brother or sister. Be certain that there are some tasks which every absent student must complete upon returning from an absence. Writing an essay or journal entry, reading and reporting on an article related to a missed class discussion, or presenting a current event are some possible independent assignments.

A list of essay subjects and a collection of articles can be kept in a file in the classroom. The important feature here is to provide assignments which do not compute into the student's grade. Collect the assignment, but you needn't worry about grading it. They have only done this work to continue to receive "practice!" Students will begin to get the message that it is easier to come to school than stay home.

As mentioned, *don't make it **easy** to be absent because an absent student does not make it **easy** on you.*

Planning for double duty

Every good teacher spends a lot of time planning and organizing lessons. A management technique that will help you save a great deal of time is to get two lessons out of each plan. The *second* plan or lesson may be taught in the next day, month, semester, or season. Regardless of when you present the material, the planning and organizing is complete so you have saved time.

You've probably used this concept in the past with projects such as generic book reports, math worksheets, or reports on states or countries. Let's look at some different types of lesson presentations and see how to "double up" with every plan.

⏱ If you do weekly or bi-weekly sets of vocabulary lessons with your students in which they complete various activities to learn the meanings and usage of words, create worksheets that are generic. They should have eight to ten different activities such as writing sentences, drawing pictures to represent the word, listing people who represent each word, listing the different forms of the word, identifying antonyms, synonyms or rhyming words, writing a paragraph using a specified number of the words, making up a riddle or poem for the words, creating a crossword puzzle, etc.

Have your students select four or five of these activities to complete with each word list. This technique is an excellent way to provide varied activities for students at different levels. You can duplicate several sets of the worksheets at the same time and then use them week after week.

If this is too repetitive for you, make two or three generic worksheets and alternate or rotate their use throughout the year.

⏰ If you have students do collages or cut pictures out of magazines to complete art projects, you can incorporate logic lessons into this activity. When they cut out the pictures, have them save the page from which they were cut. Paste them on sheets of paper, exchange them among students, and have individuals try to imagine and then replicate the original (cut out) art work. In so doing, students are interpolating and extrapolating data -- a logic skill that is rarely part of their regular curriculum.

Once the collages are complete and have been displayed, have students cut them into the original pictures. Students can sort the pictures by attribute or create Venn diagrams.

⏰ On writing assignments, delete names and then redistribute papers randomly. Have students rewrite a classmate's paper, making corrections and additions. Staple the original and the rewrite together and return them to the original writer. He or she must then rewrite the paper combining the original and the rewrite. You might give the collaborating students a shared grade. Using this approach, students get the practice of writing, proofing, editing, and re-editing, while improving their grade and saving you planning and correcting time.

⏰ If you are designing a lesson using manipulatives in math, think of future lessons which could be taught with the same set of manipulatives. For example, if second graders were working on regrouping in addition and you planned to use color chips, Cuisinaire rods, and ice cream sticks during the two week unit, label all of their worksheets and activities "Addition and Subtraction with Regrouping." Either white out or omit the + and - symbols, duplicate twice the number of copies, and you're well on your way to planning a two week subtraction unit. You'll need to check to be sure your subtraction problems include appropriate regrouping.

This same approach can be used with addition, subtraction, multiplication and division of fractions; decimal operations; decimals and percentage; and multiplication and division. It is also applicable to activities which become increasingly complex throughout the year such as telling time, rounding and place value (decimals and whole numbers), working with money, and computing percentage.

It makes a lot more sense to spend fifteen minutes creating a worksheet which you will use three times than a worksheet you'll use once.

⊕   In the humanities, there are two approaches in applying the *two for one* concept. Most often, when we teach art, music, dance or drama in our classrooms, the focus is on "production" or performance; that is, we draw, paint, sing, play, dance, move, or act. There are other important components on which we spend much less time -- history and appreciation. By bringing the background or history of an art work to students and by interpreting or analyzing the structure of the work with the students, their "production" is enhanced. Incorporating these components into your production enables you to generate two or three lessons for one.

A second method to get two lessons for one in humanities is to prepare the same lesson for two or three presentations throughout the school year. If, for example, you are teaching American history and wish to incorporate music into your curriculum, plan to do several music components during the year. A linking topic might be *Songs of War* and you might teach the music of the *Revolutionary period*, the *Civil War*, and the songs of *World War I*. Although the songs themselves will differ, the topic is similar and allows you to use the same lesson format and follow-up materials.

If you chose to do a unit on American Painters, you might plan several short units or one each quarter. The assignment given for each painter could be the same using questions such as: How do the artist's subjects reflect the times in which he or she lived? How does the style of dress, depicted by the artist, reflect the values of America during his or her time? If the artist had painted one more picture, what do you think the subject matter would have been? Then give students a chance to paint in the style of the artist.

ⓘ At some point, you might use a checklist system for completion of some long term assignment. For example, if students were to do a science project, they might have a ten step checklist or time line to follow. Sample steps might be: (1) select topic and state thesis, (2) bring six research sources to class which represent at least four different types of resources, (3) write an opening paragraph which clearly states your topic, etc.

If you use a time line/checklist approach once during the year, plan on using it twice; perhaps once each semester. As you prepare your packet of explanation for the first topic, make it sufficiently generic to work for the second project. This can be done even if it is an assignment in a completely different subject area.

As you progress through the first unit, you may make alterations in the plan. Update and amend your unit explanation and by the second semester you will be ready with your second extensive project with very little planning required.

ⓙ If you create your own worksheets or sets of sentences for students to analyze in grammar or foreign language classes, type the sentences on a word processor. By making very subtle changes you can, in two or three extra minutes, get two sets of sentences instead of one. Simply type ten sentences, print them, make changes and print again.

1. At the store, Bill and Roger purchased their groceries.

Print this first ten sentences and then make changes for the second worksheet.

1. Bill and Jan looked in the bag at their groceries.
(second worksheet with changes)

You can use the same approach to make math worksheets, although if you apply this to math, I suggest you use a spreadsheet program. That way you can create a teacher answer sheet at the same time by using spreadsheet formulas.

If you teach geography and include map skills there are ways to do double planning. Begin by duplicating two sets of maps and give one copy to each student. After students have colored and labeled one map, and after you have discussed it with the class, have them cut out the states, countries, bodies of water, etc. and store them in an envelope to reassemble the map as they would a puzzle. Give them a day or two to work with the puzzle.

A week after they have done the first puzzle, with labels, have them do the same map without labels. They can then cut up the second map and go to work at memorizing states, continents, capitals, etc. by using labeled and non-labeled pieces interchangeably. You will not only have generated three or four lessons from one, you will also have provided experiences for your visual, auditory and kinesthetic learners.

⊕   Teaching life science, physical science and earth sciences within one school year is a challenge to almost every teacher who works in a self-contained setting. Typically you have an interest or knowledge in one of these areas but the others are less appealing. Given this predicament, work with a colleague, each of you preparing a different unit and then either sharing resources *or* teaching one another's class. In other words, if you prepare a unit on simple machines, your colleague can prepare a unit on magnetism. You teach your machine unit to two classes and your "partner" teaches the magnetism unit to both classes. This is a form of two for one planning.

     If, however, sharing is not a choice, you can approach your science curriculum from a viewpoint of how the sciences are classified and how they are interrelated. A typical third grade science curriculum might include:

Your Body's Needs	*Fossils*
Light and Sound	*Water*
Magnetism and Electricity	*Adaptation and Habitat*
The Earth and its Crust	*Understanding Plants*

     In a one hour planning period, you can generate numerous activities which can be used for each of these units. For example, you might have students list vocabulary words which would be used in discussion of each topic, list occupations or famous people within each topic, do an oral or written presentation on one occupation or person from each field, have students respond to a series of questions (i.e. Why is this science important? How might discoveries in this area affect you in the future? What would our lives be like without knowledge of this science?), organize a guest speaker or two for each topic, have each student do an experiment or project within each topic, or find a link with each topic to another aspect of your curriculum (a short story, social studies, or creative writing).

While this plan does not eliminate the need for you to prepare individual experiments for each topic, you have, in one hour of planning, organized sufficient material for at least twenty-four lessons (three days per unit). If science is not an area of strength, you probably will also do a more cohesive job of teaching science than you have ever done before.

🕐   If you're going to do an activity which you know will make a mess in your classroom, you may as well make the mess once and complete two projects at the same time. For example, if you are using plaster of Paris for a student project, figure out something you can do for a future lesson and pour that at the same time. If you are using clay that will be fired, do your individual class project but also make bowls which you can break and use for an archeological dig later in the year. If you are making globes of paper maché, make a piñata at the same time. If students are making individual relief maps with a flour, salt, and water dough, make a large version for classroom use. You get the idea...

●   ●   ●

Two for one planning is one of the best bargains in time management. It needs to become your mode of operation. You'll be amazed, once you start thinking and planning this way, every aspect of your teaching becomes more efficient and in many cases, more effective.

If you can apply all that has been discussed in this chapter, your classroom management will be the envy of your fellow teachers. When you consider the minimal amount of time required to follow through with these suggestions of planning before retiring for the evening, writing things down, mobilizing your students, cataloging your classroom, setting procedures, preparing for absentees, and doing double planning, mightn't it be worth the effort invested?

Managing
Your Discipline

Why a chapter on discipline in a time management book? If all students who walked into our classrooms were organized and goal oriented, there would be no need for books on discipline. Our jobs would be easier, our lives happier, and teaching would be a much more popular profession.

Unfortunately, this is not the case and so we spend hours dealing with and attempting to alter the behavior of students who are discipline problems. They range from non-achievers to absentees, from those who "act up" to those who won't act at all, and in the past decade to drug babies, drug users, drug sellers, and children with children. The task at times seems insurmountable, and that is where time management and planning can have an impact.

If you recall the outstanding students you've had in the past, their qualities probably included self-motivation, enthusiasm, creativity and organization. In other words, they had a strong sense of self-discipline. Time management and self-discipline go hand in hand. We just need to find a way to get students to start working on the "self."

Very few people are inherently organized and self-motivated. Time management is not natural to us. It's a skill which we must acquire. Your students are in the same position. They have to learn to set priorities, to establish goals, to have a purpose; in short, to have a plan of attack that they are willing to implement. If you can instill this sense of purpose in your students, you'll find a sharp drop in the amount of time you spend on discipline problems.

Kids *are* different now. Some generalizations identifying this difference might include: a sense of complacency, a lack of motivaiton, and a need to be entertained rather than taught. Although today's students are probably brighter and more sophisticated in their thinking, there seems to be a component lacking.

As an example, do you remember the excitement you felt when your teacher would roll the sixteen millimeter projector cart into the classroom for films? Today's students have seen it all. It seems we spend most of our time motivating students extrinsically hoping that the intrinsic (self) will follow. To motivate, we have to become entertainers, or we buy or give students something as an incentive. We need to work on the student from the inside out. That's what time management, goal setting, and this chapter are all about.

Since we are never going to eliminate all of our problems in the classroom and because society seems to keep finding new problems for kids to adopt, this chapter also presents some approaches to handling or managing the difficult students you encounter.

From my experience in the classroom, I've developed a set of twelve discipline guidelines that have worked for me both from the standpoint of classroom organization and in saving time. If you choose to use some of these ideas you will need to make adjustments to fit your personal style.

1. Be certain your disciplinary and academic expectations are realistic.

2. Respect breeds respect. Be a role model worthy of the respect of your students in demeanor, in content, and in dress.

3. Never put a student down in front of others.

4. Be certain your requirements fit your conviction.

5. Establish your personal heirarchy of consequences.

6. Attack and resolve one misbehavior at a time.

7. Work with parents. You will not win without them.

8. Make your expectations simple, clear, and consistent. Eliminate *all* grey areas.

9. Tell your students what you expect and hold them to your expectations.

10. What your students think of you today is less important than what they will think of you ten years from now.

11. Keep things in perspective by using the 80-20 rule.

12. Keep a simple anecdotal record on each student who has caused you to make three parent contacts.

Be certain your expectations are realistic

Given your grade level assignment, what types of behavior can and should you expect? How can these behaviors be modified to fit into your desired environment? Do your children have the maturity to meet your expectations physically and emotionally?

First graders will not be able to stay on task for extended periods of time no matter what you plan. Junior high school students are far more concerned about the opinion of the person on either side of them than with what you have to say. High school students will generally not respond to you unless you first establish a sense of mutual respect. Every grade level has its idiosyncrasies.

If your expectations contradict the physical and emotional stages of your students, your discipline program can't be successful. Know your audience and set your expectations at a level which is reachable by your students and by you.

Respect breeds respect. Be a role model worthy of respect in demeanor, in content, and in dress.

As teachers, we too often appear less than professional. If we want to be treated as professionals, we need to act, talk, and look like professionals to our students and to our communities.

This doesn't mean a new dress or pin stripe suit, but it does mean thorough planning, presentable clothing, grammatically correct writing, organized delivery, and effective communication.

If we want the respect of our students we must provide them with someone to look up to and to emulate. We needn't be stuffy or overly proper but we can't be "laid back" or be "buddies" with our students. Stuffiness or over-familiarity will not gain the stature of respect we need to foster every moment, every day.

Yes, there are fine lines in this discussion and there are many teachers who are well-liked and appreciated who become very familiar with their students. But, friendliness and caring are different than joining the student group.

Does an overweight physician who discusses the importance of weight loss have any credibility? Do parents who stroll in late to a conference, disheveled and unaware of what is happening in their child's life convince you that they are thoroughly committed to the welfare of their child? Quite simply, we are what we present ourselves to be; we must be role models for our students.

And what does this have to do with time management? It all goes hand in hand with the attitude we develop by being true professionals.

The time it takes to proofread a letter, do your hair, organize your day, tie a tie, arrive early to class, have all papers ready, clean off your desk, polish your shoes, post bulletin boards, press a shirt, etc., is minimal compared to the damage you do by not taking the time to present yourself, each day, as a professional.

Your presence and demeanor in your classroom sets a tone. If you do the little things to enhance the "tone," you'll not waste time trying to establish it after the fact.

Never put down a student in front of others

Most adults and most children's clearest negative remembrance of school is being embarrassed by a teacher. Sometimes things we say which seem so harmless are like darts flying through the room.

Part of our job is to correct and guide errant students, and we all have techniques for doing this in a positive way. When it gets to a strong reprimand, respect yourself and your students enough to do this one to one.

If you chastise a student or his ideas in front of peers, it may take weeks or even months of your time to regain that student's trust or respect. Don't place that burden upon yourself.

A brief word about sarcasm: a teacher should never use sarcasm when disciplining a child. Students either don't understand it and miss the point *or* they understand it and thoroughly dislike it. Joking with students is very different than teasing them or being sarcastic. Be aware where one ends and the next begins.

Be certain your requirements fit your conviction

The discipline program you establish in your classroom must be consistent with your attitudes. There's no point making a rule if you can't enforce it. Many parent conferences and many student and parent complaints can be avoided by keeping this idea in mind as you set your standards.

Establish your personal heirarchy of consequences

In establishing a consistent and organized discipline program, you need to spend some time developing a list of consequences. Some of these are dictated by school policy or practice, but it helps to have your own ideas organized as well. The benefit of having such a list is that you can handle problems as they occur. You avoid over analyzing to find the proper procedure or second guessing yourself for having done the wrong thing or reacting too strongly.

A possible heirarchy might include:

Ignore the behavior
Give the "look"
Remove from the group with a "time out" in class
Exclude from the group for a longer period of time
Conference with child

Keep in class for one minute of recess

Keep in class for three to five minutes of recess

Move desk/change seat

Take points/rewards away

Isolate in the classroom - desk away from everyone

Send out of room

Stay after school

Miss a fun or desirable activity

Hold in for entire recess/lunch

Assign extra work

Don't allow student to participate - remove the honor
of participating

Call parents

Move to another classroom for a period of time

Student writes an apology

Send to Principal or Dean of Students

Parent conference with the child present

Parent spends the day in class with the child

Refer for special testing

Suspension

Send home at lunch

Place on minimum day

You will undoubtedly be able to add some ideas as well
as change the order to fit your approach or grade level.

Three points in establishing your heirarchy: First,
never punish yourself when punishing a child. You didn't do
anything wrong! Don't give up your lunch, recess, Saturdays,
or after school hours; don't spend excessive time writing letters

to parents (some documentation is necessary, of course); don't give assignments which you must spend extra time to correct. Plan your consequences to impact the child, not the teacher.

Second, *don't expect your principal to handle your problems for you*. The more you personally take care of in class, the more respect your students -- even those being disciplined -- will have for you.

Third, *make the punishment fit the crime*. Don't be excessive in your consequences. You need to save the serious disciplines, such as suspension, parent conferences, and referrals to the principal, for serious infractions.

If you spend time to generate this list, you'll find you spend less time on discipline and better yet, you won't show your anger when a student misbehaves.

Speaking of this heirarchy, it helps to view your list of consequences as a deck of cards stacked in your favor. You don't want to give the next card away without getting full impact of the card just played. Be patient and don't expose your hand to students or to their parents.

Attack and resolve one misbehavior at a time

Changing a habit is hard work, even when you want to change. Changing a habit of a child is even harder. Research shows that it takes at least twenty-one days to unlearn or develop an habitual behavior. Since it is so hard to change, be realistic and only work on one behavior at a time. Let the student and his or her parents work with you on one identified behavior for at least a month before addressing a second fault.

For example, if you have a student who rarely does homework, is aggressive in class, and uses bad language, work with the parents to identify which of these behaviors is the most destructive. Put your efforts into altering the one behavior. Correct the others, if necessary, but focus on *changing* one at a time.

As a problem is corrected, the praise the child receives acts as a catalyst for future alterations.

Work with parents, work with parents, and then work with parents. You will not win without them.

You must win each and every parent over to your side. This is no small task but as soon as you have done this, you won't believe the time and aggravation you'll save. "An ounce of prevention is worth a pound of cure," is a cliché worth remembering. The introductions, the letters, and the contacts you make with every parent early in the year is *very* time consuming, but each minute up front saves five down the line.

Let parents know you are organized, that you care, and that you are working in the best interests of not only their child but every child in your class. Be professional in your contacts with them; clearly spell out your visitation and conference policy (i.e. no drop ins). Share your curriculum goals for the year and keep them posted at least each month with a newsletter. Explain your grading program, discipline program, and homework policy. Call them often to tell them something good their son or daughter has done. Send corrected work home with students. Ask them to volunteer in class (read about delegation in Chapter 6) and always speak in terms of being a "team" to work together to help their child.

The time you spend keeping parents informed, about all aspects of your program, will save hours and hours throughout the school year.

Make your expectations simple, clear and consistent and eliminate all gray areas.

The clearer you are in your own mind about what you want, the clearer you can be with your students. Your expectations must be simple and to the point. The fewer "rules" you have, the better. Five should be a maximum and should include reference to having all required materials at the beginning of each day, treating peers and adults with respect, refraining from the use of bad language or innuendo, respecting the property of the school and others, and taking responsibility for their own actions.

Each one of the expectations listed above is somewhat broad and needs written clarification. A sample classroom discipline letter might include:

Dear Student and Parent:

I look forward to working with your son or daughter in class this year. My goal is to provide a positive learning atmosphere for your child and every other child. To this end, I think it's important to be very clear about my expectations of their responsibilities in our classroom.

I have four rules which I expect every student to adhere to every day they are in class whether I am present or not.

1. Students must be prepared for class each day.

Students are responsible for having a pen and pencil, college ruled three hole punched paper, textbooks provided by the school, and completed homework assignments at the beginning of each school day.

Students are expected to be on time, in class, and in their seats at the beginning of each class period.

2. Students must treat their peers and adults with respect.

Name calling, racial slurs, "put downs," laughing at (as opposed to laughing with), harrassment, gestures, physical treatment and teasing will not be tolerated. A simple way for students to remember this expectation is: if you have nothing nice to say, say nothing.

3. Students must use appropriate language.

Obviously, profanity of any kind is not acceptable. In addition, I find many words which television accepts as appropriate to be inappropriate and unacceptable in my classroom. A person's backside simply need not be referred to; words which do appear in the Bible (a defense I have heard from students on occasion) when used as slang or exclamations are not acceptable; innuenedo or double meanings of words are unacceptable (teachers are not naive as many students may think). These standards apply to all written work as well.

The concept to keep in mind: if you're in doubt, don't say or use it!

4. Students must treat all school property and the property of others with respect.

Desks, chairs, classroom materials, textbooks, and all other property which does not belong to the student must be treated with care and respect. To this end, students will be held financially responsible for any damage done to other property. Materials of any kind are not to be thrown.

If a student's personal property has inappropriate markings, including profanity or graffiti, the materials will be confiscated and returned to the parents.

I provide these expectations to you to eliminate confusion. I anticipate that since this is clearly spelled out, your son or daughter will have very little trouble following the rules. I appreciate your support and ask that you and your son or daughter sign in the spaces provided, thus acknowledging that you have read and understand these expectations.

_____   _____
Student's Signature   Parent's Signature

Tell your students what you expect and hold them to your expectations.

Once you have established, communicated, and posted your expectations you must reinforce them. If you lack consistency in enforcing your standards, or if you back down when confronted by a student or parent, you may as well never have established them in the first place. Your commitment is essential.

What your students think of you today is less important than what they will think of you ten years from now.

"Deferred gratification" is my term for this concept. There are very few teachers who do not want their students to like them as people. However, sometimes they can like you but not respect you. Lack of respect is deadly.

When you were in school, did you ever have a teacher who was "nice" but taught you nothing and demanded nothing of you? A teacher who perhaps let too many things go by or was inconsistent with discipline and learning? The year may have gone smoothly with little demand and little conflict, but in the long run, it was a waste of your time.

On the other hand, did you ever have a teacher who was perhaps less "friendly," whose classroom was a bit less comfortable and more structured, who made you feel somewhat challenged with each assignment and who taught you a great deal? For whom do you have more respect as you look back? Nine out of ten adults identify the latter.

It would be ideal if every teacher had the perfect mix of kindness, consistency and fairness but unfortunately this is not possible. What do you want your students to think and to say about you five or ten years from now? You may have to defer some of the gratification of pleasing your students for the moment, but in the long run, it is worth it.

Apply the 80-20 to keep a positive perspective

The 80-20 rule is a "rule of thumb" of business which essentially says that eighty percent of your sales come from twenty percent of your customers; the inverse being that twenty percent of sales come from the remaining eighty percent of customers. Your classroom discipline problems probably follow this rule as well. That is, eighty percent of your discipline problems are generated by twenty percent of your students.

In an average classroom of thirty children, six children are going to create the majority of the problems or disturbances. A larger portion may follow along if allowed to do so, but basically, most teachers will agree that there are a few children who create most of the problems.

These students take on many attributes. They may be defiant, talkative, non-productive, absent, disrespectful, unprepared, tardy, obscene, non-motivated, insecure, humorous, or a variety of other non-endearing traits. If you don't have any of these children, wait until *next* year; if you have a classroom full of them, *wait* until next year.

Joking aside, the numbers posed by the 80-20 rule should give you some perspective and hope about the opportunity of working with twenty-four members of your class who want and are ready to learn. In other words, don't allow twenty percent to ruin your teaching day.

Easily said, yet difficult to do... yes, *but you are never going to eliminate all of your problems*. There is always a bottom rung on the ladder. If right now you could select five children to remove from your classroom, the sixth child (the one not selected) would become your biggest problem. Five (or so) more would fill the discipline void created by those who were gone. It is human nature to create this hierarchy in our minds.

Since you cannot change this dilemma, learn to work within it. Focus time and effort on those six students. Write notes and daily or weekly progress reports to their parents, get to know their parents by conferencing and through other face to face contact, visit their homes, let them know how much you want to help their child, educate your administrators as to what you are doing, correct one of their problems at a time, develop a discipline plan which the parents will support and adhere to, and most important, reward yourself when you make small "break throughs" in their performance at school.

To make this type of effort with thirty children is nearly impossible. To follow through with six students is manageable. Your efforts with your twenty percent will allow you to maintain a positive outlook with the eighty percent who *want* to learn.

Departmentalized teachers who face 180 children per day will have more parental and student contacts. Twenty percent of 180 students is many more than twenty percent of thirty students. On the positive side, the middle school, junior high or high school teacher faces each individual discipline challenge for only fifty minutes per day.

It's not a matter of whether self-contained or departmentalized is easier or more difficult. Regardless of your grade level, your twenty percent arrive every day or every hour. On the bright side, eighty percent, or four out of five students, give us a reason to do our best each day.

As mentioned previously, you will never eliminate all of your discipline problems. An applicable cliché is, "The best defense is a good offense." Be on the offense with your problem students and their parents. Don't allow yourself to be placed in a position in which you must defend your actions. Be open, be candid, be consistent, and be the initiator of an improvement program with each student and his or her parents. Your foresight and follow through can make most of your disciplinary problems at least tolerable and may become some of your greatest rewards in teaching.

Keep an anecdotal record of disciplinary, corrective, observed actions

Every student can improve. Part of our responsibility as teachers is to inspire every student to improve academically, socially, and emotionally as much as possible each year. It's unrealistic to imagine that we can actually do this; yet, it must be our goal.

To rely on your memory to recall all of the subtleties and nuances of your student's individual progress is impossible. You must record your observations. However, keeping an anecdotal record on every student is almost impossible. Keep an ongoing anecdotal record for every student who has caused you to make three parental contacts. Chances are, after three contacts with parents, with little change in behavior, the student is probably going to be an ongoing challenge. If you ever hope to enforce some of the more stringent consequences on the hierarchy of discipline procedures, an ongoing record will be essential.

The student log on the next page is one method of recording this data. Some sample comments are included. You will be surprised how useful this individual record can be as you move through a school year. And realistically, these records need only be kept on that "20%" identified earlier.

You can keep this anecdotal record in your organizer, grade book, or planning book, but wherever you choose to log your observations, keep all records in the same place.

Student Observation/Discipline Log

Student's Name: _____

Mother's Name: _____

Home Phone: _____ Work Phone: _____

Address: _____

Father's Name: _____

Home Phone: _____ Work Phone: _____

Address: _____

Other: _____

Home Phone: _____ Work Phone: _____

Address: _____

Date	Observation	Action Taken
9/15	Abe has not turned in any assignments so far this year	Called his mother who said she would check his homework each evening
10/3	Abe was in a fight with Anthony during lunch time	Sent to principal and he was suspended from school
10/7	Abe has stayed after school three times for extra help	
10/22	Abe was throwing food at lunch with Ruben and Josh	Cleaned up lunch area, and I sent note to his mother
11/2	Abe was voted student of the month by his classmates	Certificate sent home
11/15	Abe went home for lunch with his father; it's the first time I've met him.	
11/17	Abe seems very withdrawn and unresponsive. He seems to want to be left alone but he wouldn't talk to me about it.	

You'll find that at parent-teacher conference time and during phone conversations with parents, you will have meaningful insights to share. This record also acts as documentation should you ever be professionally challenged by a parent, administrator, or attorney.

The greatest challenge in teaching is managing discipline problems while attempting to motivate students to learn. The day in and day out stress created by trying to walk this fine line is what teaching is all about. It is exhausting, frustrating, demanding, and demoralizing, yet to teachers it is the *great challenge*.

As simple as it is to write about managing your time in handling your disciplinary problems, it is equally as difficult to bring all of these ideas to a working level. They are presented for your consideration. However, if you are ever going to be a true manager of your time, implementing a structured and organized discipline plan is an essential component.

There's No Substitute
for Teaching

Many teachers begin their careers as substitute teachers. Whether or not you have had the experience of walking into an unfamiliar classroom every day, it seems that we all share a certain amount of empathy for these underpaid and underappreciated colleagues. There is one advantage to being a substitute in that he or she can say "no" on any given day. It's a luxury which is not available to the regular classroom teacher. They provide a vital service but at times place us in one of our most difficult dilemmas -- a dilemma which you probably discovered sometime during your first or second year of teaching.

You know the scenario... you awaken in the morning feeling ill and you conduct a soliloquy:

"I don't feel well, I think I'll call a sub."
      "But I have nothing planned."

"The way I feel I'll never make it through the day."
      "I have to call a sub."

"I'll just have the sub call when he/she gets to school and go over lesson plans."
"I don't have my books to do plans."

"I really don't feel well."
"If I go to school, maybe I'll feel better."
"What should I do?"

Eventually, you made one of two possible decisions. You got dressed and suffered through the day at school, or you called a sub and spent part of your morning trying to think of plans which were easy to prepare and which your class could handle, and then suffered through the remainder of the day worrying about how things were going. Neither solution was beneficial to your condition.

If this scene was or is familiar to you, there is a solution at hand. It involves some revolutionary thinking and a few hours of planning, but if you are willing to give it a try, *this will be the last planning you will ever do for a substitute teacher.*

Your absence throws things off kilter for your children and for you. Regardless of the thoroughness of your plans, it generally takes one day for each day of sub time just to bring your students back to where they were when you left. Most teachers agree that staying home is usually more of a hassle than coming to school, but since there will be times that you will need to stay home, we begin by establishing the role of your substitute.

1. Your substitute is a REVIEWER -- no new material.
2. Your sub plans are UNIVERSAL -- for this year and every year.
3. Your sub leaves you NOTHING TO CORRECT.

There is no reason for your substitute to present new material to your children. Nine times out of ten, you will feel uncomfortable with or unsure of what has been done, and you'll go back and reteach it anyway. Use your sub as a *reviewer*. It makes it easier for the sub because all students have already covered the material, and it is easier for students because we are not instigating a possible *relearning* process.

Forget the cooperative learning seating, forget the reading groups, and the involved organizational plans that you normally use. You are probably the only one who can figure them out anyway. Your sub should only review information previously taught.

Your sub plans should be *universal*, regardless of time of day, time of year, or the suddenness of your illness. Your preparation should have the same format and types of activities within a set framework with only the activities changing from one sub day to the next.

All activities presented by your sub are either *self-correcting* or *non-correcting*. You should let your sub know, in the standard letter that you will be writing, that this is your goal. The premise is that students will correct their work and will take all of their work home with them at the end of the day. It is important that your return to the classroom is spent in reinstituting your program. A stack of papers, collected the previous day, will only deter you from getting back into the "flow" of teaching.

A second benefit of the self-correcting approach is that it provides closure throughout the day for your class. A substitute teacher upsets the students' equilibrium for the day. The cycle of doing an assignment and then correcting it is comfortable and natural. It eliminates uncertainty. It also allows a "fresh" start every fifteen to forty-five minutes. A good substitute can use this as a motivational tool.

Now, we move on to the actual preparation of the substitute file.

First, you'll need to write your "last" letter to a substitute teacher. In this letter, you are going to include all of the information listed below (for the entire year). If you have a word processor to work on, it's a good idea to use it so you can change the dates when you get next year's duty schedules. For your convenience, two sample letters are provided. The first for a self-contained teacher, the second for a departmentalized teacher.

1. Your name, your principal's name, your aide's name and the name of the teacher next door
2. The universal class schedule
3. Seating chart
4. Where to find and how to use sub folders
5. Where to find coffee and eat lunch (that homey touch).
6. The duty schedule
7. Procedures (to include)
   (a) attendance and tardies
   (b) students entering and leaving the classroom
   (c) use of bathrooms
   (d) lunch procedures
   (e) what students do when they have finished assignments
   (f) special schedules
   (g) location of daily and weekly bulletins
   (h) discipline plan

A Sample Substitute Letter: Self-contained

Dear Substitute:

Good morning! My name is Scott Purdy and this is a fourth grade classroom. I have a three hour aide from 8:30 until 11:30 and her name is Joan Green. She will be very helpful in answering any questions you may have. Our principal's name is Bob Raleigh. If you have any problems with students, let him know and he will be in to talk with them. The teacher next door is Martha Enright.

There is hot water available in the teachers' lounge and there is also a refrigerator and microwave available for your use. Most of the teachers eat lunch there and you are welcome to join them. I've left a clean coffee mug and some packets of instant coffee in the bottom drawer of my desk. Please help yourself!

In the top drawer of the gray file cabinet you will find several folders marked SUBSTITUTE - DAY 1, DAY 2, etc. This letter is universal so I'm not certain which day was used last so just take the first full folder in line.

As you will see, the day is broken into 15 to 45 minute segments. There is an activity for each time span. My goal is to return to school tomorrow and see only your notes about the children's behavior. Students will be correcting their own work. I have already spoken to them about the procedure and they know that all the activities are to be done with the entire class. The approach will not be new to them.

● Attendance should be taken first thing in the morning. Write the names of absent students on a slip of paper and place it on the clip by the front door. Students who come in later than five minutes after the beginning of class must check in at the office.

● When students enter the room they are to do so quietly. They will line up outside the door and will enter when you ask them.

● A student who leaves the room needs to sign on the chalkboard when leaving and erase it upon return. Only one student may be out of the room at a time.

● During lunch, the children know where they are to eat and the location of their play area. You have no duty during the lunch period (12:00 -12:45).

● When students finish assignments they should keep their papers at their desks and read their library books. Students should have books in their desks. There is reference to this in the daily plan.

● We have several special classes which we attend. You will need to walk the students to these activities but you have no responsibilities for supervision while at the activity. They are as follows:

Monday -	Library (11:00 - 11:30)
Tuesday -	Music (11:00 - 11:30) / P.E. (1:00 1:30)
Wednesday -	Computer (10:00 - 10:30)
Thursday -	P.E. (1:00 - 1:30)
Friday -	No special activities

● Please check the weekly bulletin (on the clipboard on the side of my desk) and the daily bulletin (in my mailbox) for other special events.

● I have morning yard duty during the weeks of 10/3, 11/23, 1/5, 2/23, 4/2, 5/15, and 6/10. You will need to cover this duty from 9:50 to 10:10.

In terms of discipline, the classroom rules are clearly posted on the front board. The students and I have discussed these rules many times so regardless of claims of, "I didn't know," students do know. We use assertive discipline as the basis for our discipline program. For the first infraction, the name goes on the board; second infraction, a check by the name, etc. I would like you to copy the names and checks down at the end of the day and I will talk with these students. If any student becomes particularly unruly, the student should be sent to Mr. Raleigh.

Here is a breakdown of the school day. You will need to adjust times for any special classes:

8:30 - 8:45	Attendance, introduce yourself, and make certain that each student has a library book. There are many books in the library in the front of the room. Get a commit ment from students that when they finish their assignments, they will read their books.
8:45 - 9:15	Activity 1
9:15 - 9:45	Activity 2
9:45 - 9:50	Clean-up jobs
9:50 - 10:10	Recess
10:10 - 10:45	Activity 3
10:45 - 11:30	Activity 4
11:30 - 11:55	Activity 5
11:55 - 12:00	Clean up jobs
12:00 - 12:45	Lunch
12:45 - 1:00	Read aloud from class reading book
1:00 - 1:45	Activity 6
1:45 - 2:15	Activity 7
2:15 - 2:45	Letters to parents explaining the day. Each activity should be a separate paragraph (or sentence) and will be the cover page of the work they take home. Please follow the correct letter writing format.
2:45 - 3:00	Clean up jobs and organize packets going home

This is a very nice group of children and I'm certain that your day will be very enjoyable.

Sincerely,

A Sample Substitute Letter: Departmentalized

Dear Substitute:

Good morning! My name is Scott Purdy, and this is a seventh-eighth grade classroom. Our principal's name is Tim Matthews and his office is in the library. If you have any problems with students, let him know, and he will to talk with them. The teacher next door is Debbie Gray.

Please feel free to use my coffee maker to heat water or make coffee. There are paper cups, sugar, tea, etc. on the shelf behind the first sliding whiteboard. There is a refrigerator and microwave available for your use in the teachers' lounge. Most of the teachers eat lunch there, and you are welcome to join them.

In the top file drawer, directly across the room from my desk, you will find several folders marked DAY 1, DAY 2, etc. This letter is universal so I'm not certain which day was used last so just take the first full folder in line.

My goal is to return to school tomorrow and see only your notes about the students' behavior. Students will be correcting their own work. I have already spoken to them about the procedure and they know that all the activities are to be done with the entire class. The approach will not be new to them.

Attendance should be taken first thing in the morning. You will find seating charts on the front counter (I have assigned seats for periods one, four, and five only). Write the names of absent students on a slip of paper (top drawer of my desk) and place it on the clip by the door (first hour only). Students who come in later than five minutes after the beginning of class must check in at the office.

A student who leaves the room needs to ask permission. Only one student to the bathroom at a time but I always allow them to go when they ask.

When students finish assignments they should keep their papers at their desks and then work on journal rewrites (they know about this).

Please check the weekly bulletin (somewhere near this letter) and the daily bulletin (in my mailbox) for other special events.

I have duty as follows: Week of . . .

September 16:	Lunch	January 22:	Second Recess
September 30:	Recess	February 10:	Bus
October 7:	Lunch	February 18:	Lunch
October 21:	Morning	March 3:	First Recess
October 28:	Second Recess	April 1:	Lunch
November 12:	Lunch	April 7:	Second Recess
November 18:	Bus	April 14:	Morning
November 25:	Lunch	April 21:	Lunch
December 9:	First Recess	April 28:	Bus
January 6:	Lunch	May 19:	First Recess
January 20:	Morning	May 26:	Lunch

In terms of discipline, the classroom rules are simple. Be prepared, show respect for the teacher and one another, listen when the teacher is talking. For infractions, use an overhead pen to make a mark on the seating chart; second infraction, a second check by the name, etc. If any student becomes particularly unruly, the student should be sent to Mr. Matthews

Before beginning each class, please read the following statement:

"In my absence today, you have a substitute. I expect better than excellent behavior from each and every one of you. In anticipation of this, you each will receive five bonus point for the class period. Should the substitute have to talk to you, individually, you lose your five. If there is a second problem, you are minus five; a third problem, well, you don't want to know because it won't happen! Have a good day and behave as you know you should. I'll see you tomorrow."

Here is a breakdown of the school day.

8:30 -	9:15	First Hour	Writing 7th/8th grade
9:15 -	10:02	Second hour	Spanish - all 8th grade
10:02 -	11:15	Prep and recess	
11:15 -	11:54	Fourth hour	Writing - 7th/8th grade
11:54 -	12:40	Fifth hour	Writing - 7th/8th grade
12:40 -	1:15	Lunch	
1:15 -	2:00	Sixth hour	Open Mind (alternating classes each day)
2:00 -	2:50	Seventh hour	Writing - same group of 8th graders as second hour

I hope you have a good day and enjoy working with the students.

Yours truly,

Scott Purdy

Since these letters are rather lengthy, it is a good idea to underline or highlight essential information. Many times a sub arrives right as the bell rings, and there is no time to read a two page letter. Highlighting helps the sub get started.

I also recommend that primary teachers maintain standard procedures at the beginning of school and after recess and lunch. If you do a "rug" activity each morning, plan this in the sub packet. If daily oral language is an after recess activity, leave this as part of your plan; if sustained silent reading or reading aloud always occurs after lunch, make this part of the plan. Younger children have better days when things begin in a more "normal" way with the sub.

One final point -- if you decide to use the bonus point concept in a self-contained classroom, I suggest you offer bonus point opportunities in blocks of time. Offer five points between the opening of school and recess, five between recess and lunch, and five from after lunch until the end of the day. This gives students a chance to "redeem" themselves if they get off to a bad start.

Thus far, I've referred to "sub folders" several times yet haven't explained the concept. To prepare them, you will need ten manila file folders. They should label them "Substitute Day One," through "Substitute Day Ten."

In each folder you will place materials to be used during the day. Therefore, you will need ten variations (one for each sub day) for each of the different activity periods as described in the substitute letter.

Ideally, it would be nice to prepare ten sub folders; however, when you first begin this program, I recommend you begin with three or perhaps four days of sub plans. With time, you can build up to ten folders

The next few pages give twenty "sure-fire" ideas for whole class activities. They are universal and should provide many avenues for finding or creating ten days of substitute lessons. There are adjustments that you will want to make for your grade level and your class. All you need to do is select some ideas you like, find resources to create ten lessons from each idea, duplicate them, and place them in your ten sub folders. Have your classroom aide or a parent volunteer do the duplicating and organizing.

① Duplicate copies of plays from basal readers, anthologies, or save sets of old Weekly Reader magazines. Assign parts to students. They love to read plays aloud and it's easy to find ten plays.

Map skills offer wonderful review possibilities as whole class activities. There are many map books available. Students can do anything from coloring the states to finding state capitals and cities to doing a map of the world. There are latitude and longtitude lessons as well. Even high school students benefit from a simple review such as coloring a U.S. map. You will be amazed what they don't know, and they can do the activity time and time again.

Write letters to famous people. Each lesson might be a letter to different types of personalities, i.e. authors, movie stars, musical performers, scientists, etc. Students should do a rough draft and final copy. They won't be sent, but the fun is in the writing.

Spelling lessons and practice on specific skills can be a good review lesson. Teaching spelling rules such as, words with two vowels, adding "y" or "s" to root words or spelling words with the "gh" sound are some possibilities. Look through old spelling books for ideas and lists of words. Have the students generate a list and then write a story using as many of the list words as possible.

Is there a student in the world who can't use handwriting and penmanship practice? Twenty to thirty minutes of practice each time a sub arrives is a natural whole class activity. Have students copy a paragraph from their library books or the sub might do a structured lesson on letter formation with students practicing.

🕐   Do a collage on a theme such as: the closest holiday, the weather, man-made machines, nature, etc. You'll need to tell the sub where to find magazines, scissors, and glue.

🕑   Read a story aloud and have students do illustrations. You might even coordinate this so you can have a sequence of pictures which students can follow as you read the story aloud a second time. It's easy to find ten such stories and it's a good idea to keep two or three such collections at your desk at all times -- just in case. Or you may want to duplicate a copy of the story for the sub and leave it in the folder.

🕒   Duplicate a page or two of math review problems (along with the answers). There is an overabundance of this material.

🕓   Do a measurement activity in which the students measure ten to fifteen different items in the room in feet, inches, or yards, and then make conversions. Conversions can be made to fractional parts of an inch as well.

🕔   Draw a top view map of the classroom, school, neighborhood, backyard, etc. Students need to draw top views several times before they really understand the concept. For younger children, leave a plastic mat and have the sub place random items on the mat. Students circle their chairs around the mat and draw the images from a top view.

🕕   Give the students a list of 8 to 10 vocabulary words to look up in the dictionary. Discuss the meanings of the words as a class and them have them write sentences or a short story using the words. Have students read their paragraphs aloud upon completion.

🕐 Duplicate copies of fairy tales, fables, or some other "classic" literary style to be read aloud with the children and to be discussed as a class.

🕐 Display an art print or two by a famous artist and have students discuss why they like or dislike the paintings or how the two paintings differ. Have them write a paragraph explaining the paintings or write a story about the people (scene). Have them read their stories to the class when they are finished.

🕐 Have a set of road maps available and have students plan a sightseeing trip through one of the states. They should include points of interest, number of miles travelled, where they will stop to spend the night, and perhaps include the total cost of lodging, food, and gas for the trip.

🕐 If your students are familiar with outlining, give them a short, factual article to outline and then go over completed outlines together as a class. This is an excellent skill for finding the main idea, finding important topics and supporting facts, and organizing factual information.

🕐 Have students think of an animal, flower, geographical location, item used in a house, etc. for each letter of the alphabet. Or, you may want them to generate a list of items and then place these items into alphabetical order.

🕐 Divide students into teams of four and give each group an everyday item such as a coathanger, a block, a dowel, or a cone, and have them work together to generate a list of ten to twenty uses for this item. Share the uses with their classmates.

⏲ Interview a classmate on a particular subject such as, My Favorite Vacation, My Favorite Toy, or My Pet Peeve. Make certain that students ask the questions: what, where, when, why, who and how, and then do an oral presentation in which they tell about the interviewed friend.

⏲ Write directions to explain some simple, everyday task. Most students have already done "How to Tie Your Shoes," but not things like How to Thread a Needle, How to Change a Bike Tire, How to Eat a Hamburger, How to Put on a Jacket, How to Open a Letter, or How to Bathe a Dog. These explanations should be explicit and step by step.

⏲ Graphing activities are a natural for a substitute and students generally enjoy making graphs. You can use pre-packaged duplicating masters or you might let students generate their own data to create a graph.

●   ●   ●

Of course, these ideas need to be dressed up or dressed down, depending upon your grade level. Primary teachers could use many of these ideas as "rug" activities in which students collectively generate the story or list with the teacher writing on the board. Students can then copy the story or use the ideas to create their own version.

Junior high and high school departmentalized teachers will only need to plan for each class period and will be able to repeat the same activity depending upon the subject and age level. A recommendation for secondary teachers is to plan two or three activites per class period -- perhaps an assignment, a second assignment, and then correction of assignments as a group. You might also use one of the writing activites and then have volunteers read their stories aloud to the class. The final activity each class period should be correcting or sharing to provide an "ending" (closure) to the lesson.

Do you have reservations as to how it would work? Try it next time you are ill.

Spend an hour this weekend gathering some materials that fit in the with the twenty ideas or create your own. Write a sub letter and *most importantly*, tell your class what will be happening.

If you are still skeptical, you might stage a practice sub day in which you and your class imagine that you are a sub. You will probably find that the seven activities that were outlined in the sub letter can be cut to five because correcting everything will take longer than you expect. You might even find that after a practice day, your children will look forward to having a substitute teacher for a day. Wouldn't that make the, "Will I or won't I," syndrome a thing of the past?

If you're ready to buy into this program right now, you'll save time. It will take an hour or two to prepare for one day of experimentation. It will take four or five hours to prepare for ten days -- less time if you have a parent or aide do your duplicating for you.

All you need are ten folders, a letter to your sub, and the organization of the activities to be done during each identified block of time. This final step is simplified if activity 1 (in each of the ten folders) is similar, and activity 2 ideas are similar, and so on through the remainder of the school day.

It's easy, it's thorough, it's a good plan for your class, and it is the last planning you will ever do for a substitute.

Try it, and save some time.

Technology

If you have ever had a grade book program crash, had sixteen millimeter film jam a projector, had a video cassette not work in the classroom (after it worked perfectly at home the night before), been unable to find the TV you signed up for at school, *lost* that word processing file you saved, had your printer break down at the "critical" time, had your overhead projector bulb burn out during class, or searched in vain for an extension cord, you understand the frustration that technology can present.

Teachers exhibit a wide range of emotions when the word *technology* arises at a staff meeting. At virtually every school, an array of reactions surface, from staunch supporters to cynical detractors. Pro or con, the reality is that computers, laser disks, CD-ROM, videocassette, networking and the internet are part of today's classrooms and will become more important every year.

If you are not a "technical/technology" person, please read this chapter with an open mind. There are many applications which take little know-how yet provide substantial time savings. Start small and keep it simple, and you'll find that some of these electronic gadgets can provide interesting opportunities for your students that are above and beyond what we are typically able to offer.

For those of you who are fascinated with gadgets, inventions, and the latest release of new computer software, your classrooms probably feature several of the ideas presented here. However, if you are like most teachers, shrinking school budgets, vandalism, theft, and minimal personal discretionary funds have probably dampened your ability to do all that you want with technology in the classroom. There are some ideas presented below which are relatively inexpensive yet rich with time saving implications.

One final observation (perhaps personal) concerns a more long range effect of technology in general. There seems to be a growing backlash to technological advances. Computer games, television, and video rentals are occupying our children's minds with passive and non-productive endeavors. Just as technology can help us in the classroom, it can also be overused. We need to make certain that the ideas presented in this chapter are used for educational benefit, not time fillers to be spent correcting or disassociating yourself from students.

Technology has opened doors which have never been available before. If we use it effectively, it can be of tremendous benefit to our students in addition to being a great time saver for us.

Cassette recorders

If you have been teaching for a number of years, you have probably used cassettes in your classroom; however, with the advent of CD's, the cassette tape is becoming a classroom dinosaur. From a time management standpoint, the cassette tape is a time saver wihtout parallel. They are recordable on inexpensive machines, child-proof, dependable, compact, and there are thousands of useful cassette tapes available for purchase.

You probably have a cassette player-recorder in your classroom; if not, you should think about purchasing a durable model with record and playback features. A built-in microphone and speakers are definitely worth the extra cost if you use some of the ideas to be presented.

If security is a problem at your school, buy an inexpensive set of speakers and have them bolted to the wall of your classroom. Run speaker wires to your desk and attach them to a jack which will plug into the headphone jack of your small recorder. With larger speakers, a machine as small as a Walkman™ can produce plenty of sound to fill your classroom so all students can hear.

Carry your cassette player back and forth to school in your purse or briefcase and security is no longer an issue. Once you are "wired" for sound, there are a variety of uses for the cassette recorder.

If you read aloud to children, have some of your best readers (or you) pre-record readings. Read chapters of ten to fifteen minute segments and write down tape numbers so you can locate the correct place at a later time. Rather than you, personally, reading the story aloud after lunch or recess (or whenever), put on the tape for children to listen to. This will free up that ten minute period to settle recess or lunch problems, talk to a student or two who need some one to one time, or to hand out materials for the next learning session. If you want to provide a professional touch, play some soft music in the background while you record your reading.

It takes time to record a book, but once you have read the book one time, it can be used year after year. Students who are absent can listen on headphones to a part of the story that they have missed.

If you are hesitant to invest this kind of time, hire a retired person to do your reading for you. It obviously must be a person who reads well and clearly, but many retired people would enjoy having such a project to work on for fifteen minutes each day. If necessary, offer to pay them for their services. Ten to twenty dollars is a token amount for the time they will invest, but it demonstrates the value of their services and your conscience will probably remain clear by offering to pay them. *The ten minutes you save each day will provide thirty hours of extra time each year.*

During visits to bookstores in the past few years, you have probably noticed the proliferation of novels and self-help books on tape. The slogan, "Have you listened to a good book lately?" is apropos. There are thousands of novels and children's books on tape. They are usually abridged editions, but they still give the entire plot and character development which you'll find in the unabridged version.

The price of these cassettes is moving down as demand has created mass markets. You can purchase a pre-recorded novel for as little as $4.95. There is also a burgeoning rental business in the *audio tape* market.

If the price of books on tape seems high, split the tape library with a friend. If you buy one book and a fellow teacher buys another, you will have a two-for-one deal that is a win for both of you.

Another use of the cassette recorder that might be considered more of a management technique than a time saver is to use it as a *mood creator* in your classroom. Playing soft harp, flute, guitar, or piano music as children enter the room has a calming effect. Playing music in the background while you do some of the mundane "first thing in the morning" tasks is a good technique.

You can also play soft music as the students are working independently. If you experiment with different types of music and observe student's behavior, you'll realize the power music holds in establishing classroom atmosphere.

A very powerful use of the cassette recorder is described in the chapter on grading (on page 36 - using a cassette to carry on a dialogue with a student as you correct his or her essay). An extension of this idea is to use cassettes to record, rather than write, lessons or messages to parents or students.

For example, in many schools, if a student is going to miss more than two or three days of class, the student is placed on independent study. The teacher must provide work for the student to do while he or she is absent. Rather than writing all of this down, simply record the assignments on cassette and give the student the tape to listen to. It is *much* faster to *tell* the assignment than to *write* it. If your district requires that the independent study must be written, tell the student (on tape) that part of the indpendent study requirements is to write down the directions you have given and to attach it to the top of the packet of completed work.

There are other ways of using the cassette as a communication device. When a student is having a difficult time understanding a specific concept in class, you can record a explanation -- to the point of referring to pages or lines in a text -- and let the student listen to the tape at home. In using this technique, I've found it to be faster and every bit as effective as sitting down with a student, one to one, to explain a difficult concept. To take this idea one step further, we often overwhelm students with information when we meet with them face to face. My experience is that most students can benefit from a recording of the one on one meeting. They can take the tape home and listen to it over and over. I use this method constantly, and the student (and parent) response is overwhelmingly positive.

You can also use the cassette recorder to have students record their work for you so you may listen to it as you drive to work. While you can't use this all of the time, why not have three to five students read (record) their essays on tape and hand them in as a "verbal" assignment? As you drive to or from school, listen to the tapes on your car stereo and record your comments on your "Walkman." It's an interesting change of pace for your students and time saver which is worth trying.

The cassette tape can also save time in preparing packets of work for students who are legitimately absent for a long period of time. Staple the student's work together and record the directions page by page. Insert positive comments like, "We miss you and hope to see you back at school soon," while explaining the student's work. You can "say" three to four times as much as you can write in a given amount of time.

The microcassette recorder

These "mini" tape recorders range in price from $30.00 to $200.00 but give the advantage of complete portability. This credit card sized wonder is small and lightweight enough to carry around in a pocket.

When you are driving to work, on duty on the playground, or waiting in a line, you can record (dictate) letters, tests, goals, thoughts, plans, etc.

You can also use the recorder to make "verbal" note of vocabulary words or specific information as you read. Making student worksheets or follow-up materials is simplified because you needn't go back and search through the text. All of the infomation is contained "on tape."

Microcassettes usually have a built in microphone so there are no external cords. You can, if you choose, use a small earphone to listen to your messages, privately.

On the negative side, microcassettes have poor sound reproduction, pose the problem of battery replacement, and offer no pre-recorded microcassettes.

Once you have become accustomed to having a microcassette recorder close at hand, you will find it a very personal and private medium which you can use to enhance your time effectiveness. It's a gadget which is dependable, compact, universal, and affordable.

Video cassette players -- VCR

Who would have thought, twenty years ago, that the video cassette business would be the billion dollar industry it is today? There is so much available to enhance your teaching that you cannot ignore this technology. Use of these tapes, both prerecorded and those recorded at home, can prove to be a tremendous time saver.

In your teaching career, how much time have you spent getting ready to show sixteen millimeter films? If you've been teaching for more than fifteen years, you probably remember them well...

...wheel in the projector, rewind the film, try to get it tracked in the sprockets with the right sized "loop," pull down the screen -- which won't roll up or won't stay down -- turn out the lights and listen to a sound track that warbles between a voice that sounds like the chipmunks one minute and Darth Vader the next, while the picture flickers on the screen.

Exaggerated? Yes, but not much. Fortunately, you probably haven't touched one of these projectors for the past five years. Sixteen millimeter has gone the way of eight track tapes and records. They represent an extinct technology.

VHS tapes are everywhere. Almost all public libraries have video catalogues from which orders can be made. Universities and county offices of education often have lending libraries. Many video stores have a section of educational video cassettes, and some even loan these tapes, free of charge, to teachers. There are numerous sources but you may have to do some searching to uncover them.

As easy as renting or borrowing videos may be, it can get frustrating from an availability standpoint. Everyone wants Pilgrim films the same week, and there's no guarantee that you will have access to the tape you want at the right time.

The solution is to create your own video library. Television has an abundance of interesting programs. The Public Broadcasting System (PBS), the Discovery Channel, the Disney Channel, and many others offer high quality programs for children. Most of this programming can be recorded for classroom use. You'll be surprised at the library you can create in a relatively short period of time.

If you begin to build your own video library, record each program on a different video cassette. If you've ever tried to find the beginning of a program in the middle of a tape with thirty children watching, you understand why it's easier to use a new tape for each program. Using a new tape each time is more expensive but the extra $2.00 is probably worth it!

You can also build your video library by borrowing and recording cassettes from colleagues. This is not to condone infringement upon the copyright laws which forbid unauthorized duplication; however, many, in fact most, recordings taken from television can be re-recorded for private, non-income generating use, without violating copyright statutes.

To record an existing cassette you need two video machines. With a little wiring magic from outputs on one machine to inputs on the other, you can make a duplicate copy. You can buy this "patch cord" setup at any electronics or stereo appliance store. Some quality is lost in the transfer, but the benefit of having your own personal copy at the precise time and place of need is worth this trouble.

Generally speaking, you know what subjects and what units you will be teaching from year to year, so begin building your video library for classroom use. Don't loan them out to teachers in grade levels above and below yours. You have gone to the trouble of recording them, so you should have the pleasure of allowing your kids to see them in your class.

What has all of this to do with time management? If you have video material which is relevant to your curriculum, is accessible when you need it, and is interesting to children, it makes sense to use class time to watch it. And if you are watching a video, you are not generating any work to correct, you have not had to prepare worksheets, and your follow-up materials can be a class discussion. Using video appropriately is the epitome of time efficiency.

One final point: your classroom should not and must not become the local movie theater. Renting a movie to "fill" ninety minutes of class time is irresponsible and unprofessional. On the other hand, an excellent show on nature or a play dramatizing a novel you have read in class can be a great enhancement to your curriculum.

Computers

The most notable technology available for your use is the computer. Many teachers have computers in their classrooms or have access to a computer lab of some type at school, and most teachers have a personal computer at home.

Grade book programs, progress reports to parents, typed tests, clip art additions, letters and worksheets, letter perfect flyers and newsletters, proof reading practice for students, and calendar programs are merely the start of possible applications.

There are numerous grade book programs on the market now. Unfortunately, many of the programs that came out in the early days of computing were not very dependable. In those days, one "crashed" program the day before report cards was all it took to put the computer away and go back to paper and pencil recording of grades.

There are many reliable and easy to use programs available now with such features as: accounting for bonus points and extra credit, zeroes (for work not received), weighted grades, and special notes to parents.

Talk to the local computer enthusiasts on your staff and find out what is available. Avoid programs that are more than three years old (I've had my own bad experiences). In software, newer is usually better.

The key to being effective with your grade book program is to *stay up to date* and *print a hard copy **every time*** you enter grades. You should (famous last words) make backup copies of your disk as well. You will be surprised how little argument there is about grades when you give students a biweekly or monthly update of averages. The computer makes this a snap.

Realistically, you'll not save time with the entry of grades since you can write them as fast as you can type them. But when you have to average grades at the end of a quarter, or when you have a parent conference scheduled right after school and need "hard" data, you just press a few keys and grades are automatically averaged and printed. You will have a complete alphabetical list of students, their individual grades, selected comments, and grade averages. Generating report card grades becomes a ten minute operation.

An alternative to a grade book program is adapting a spreadsheet program. You'll sacrifice some of the "customized" extras of grade programs, but spreadsheets are standard software equipment with most computers sold these days. Spreadsheets come in many forms and from many companies, but regardless of the software you have, you can adapt it to function as your grade book.

Word processors are capable of saving thousands of hours over the course of a teacher's career. Teaching is repetitive to a degree; we do the same types of activities each year with minor additions or adjustments to the curriculum. In my experience, I am still reusing letters and lesson follow-up materials which I created eight years ago. The material has undergone a metamorphosis since the first year, but it has only been a matter of retyping bits and pieces each year to update these files. If you use your computer, you can call up last year's files, make slight revisions and have a printed copy in no time.

In addition to the benefits of easily accessible and changeable files, another value of computer word processing is it helps us attain *perfection* in the mechanics of our writing. As professionals, we must be absolutely certain that every paper we hand out is letter perfect -- this is especially true of any letter we send home to parents. We do a disservice to ourselves and our profession when we allow any error to be seen by our students or parents. Use the word processor's spell check, thesaurus, and editing features to ensure that the work we distribute is as error free as possible. You should also have a colleague or spouse proofread your letter after spell check; inevitably there is one more mistake.

When you are learning to use a word processor, hire someone to teach you your specific program. It needn't be a professional; in fact, there are many students who could become your computer tutor (interesting reversal here). You will spend many wasted hours trying to learn from a manual or by experimenting on your own.

If you pay someone who knows about computers, you will find that it is money well spent. You will learn in one hour what would have taken eight hours to decipher. You might even work a trade. For example, if you'll teach me the computer, I'll bake you a batch of chocolate chip cookies!

In addition to grade books and word processing, there are a number of programs on the market which will allow you to create banners, flyers, awards, greeting cards and other computer generated goodies. You have probably seen the results or samples of these specialty programs.

The beauty of working with this type of computer program is that *your students can do the design and printing*. The programs are easy to operate and the results can be stunning.

First grade students can create simple greeting cards, posters, and banners, and high school students can do remarkable things with graphic design. You, the teacher, do nothing more than give the students the information and a purpose and let them create.

There are *numerous* editing programs available on computer for student use. These programs move far beyond spell checking and use of a thesaurus. I have used an editing program with my students which cost $49.00 and checks for items such as...

Active versus passive voice

Topic sentences within paragraphs

Number of sentences per paragraph

Correct use of homonyms and homophones

Split infinitives

Double negatives

Use of subject versus object pronouns

Correct use of comparatives and superlatives

The program does not make changes for students, it prompts them to decide whether or not a change is necessary. It gives examples of proper usage versus sub-standard usage and talks about the concept of *audience*.

This program represents individualized learning through technology at its best. From a time saving standpoint, when the teacher receives a paper from the student who has worked through the suggested corrections in this computer program, making final comments and grading time is cut by at least fifty percent. It reverts to the *two for ten* principle. It takes some time to learn to use the program, but it saves lots of time in the future.

The calendar programs on computer are fun to use and are excellent time savers in terms of organization, presentation, and communication. The newer programs, which sell for less than $20.00, will allow you to print out yearly, monthly, weekly, or daily calendars and organizers.

They are easy to use and provide an excellent means of teaching time management skills to your students. You can print a weekly list of homework assignments, a monthly list of due dates for a project, a listing of class activities for the month, daily lists of the class schedule (excellent for helping absentees get caught up), monthly newsletters to parents, and student organizers in which they can write their daily and long-term homework assignments.

Students can learn to use these programs and can do much of your work for you if you delegate the responsibility to them.

CD ROM

A CD ROM disk has revolutionized computer use. Many teachers have begun to create their own CD's of sample student work, models of student writing, and visual explanations of concepts taught in class. We're only seen the tip of the iceberg with this technology.

Some examples of the types of discs which are available include: an entire encyclopedia (pictures and all) on one five inch disc; the phone book for the entire United States on one disc; or the complete Webster's dictionary, Roget's Thesaurus, rhyming dictionary, Atlas, and Bartlett's Book of Quotations on one disc. The best part of all is the cost -- computer CD's are available by the thousands at prices as low as $5.00.

Obviously, it is a very powerful and compact technology. There are literally hundreds of teacher applications available, and more are being added every day.

In terms of saving time in your teaching career, it will make it far easier to collect quantities of information, have sources instantly available to students, find resources instantaneously, and keep your room much cleaner and more organized by saving massive amounts of paper storage. It is a technological advancement that rivals the cassette tape in terms of power and ease of use.

Begin learning about the CD ROM technology. It will make your life as a teacher easier.

Whether you are a believer or skeptic when it comes to the value of technology in education is almost immaterial. The children in our classrooms live in a world in which electronics and computers are the standard. They are the ones who know how to program the VCR's, load software in their computers, set the alarm on their digital watches to ring in the middle of class, buy the latest CD to listen to on their portable CD players, and score 10,000 points on the latest computer game.

If we don't join with them in appreciating this technology, they will move past us and leave us in the dust. Technology can save you time and stress. It can make you a better and more interesting teacher. You owe it to yourself to learn to use it to your advantage.

25 Time Saving Ideas

Being time efficient doesn't mean that you must become a "minute counter," trying to pack as much into each moment as possible. Time efficiency means *having time to do what you want to do by efficiently completing what you have to do*. From my teaching perspective, the "have to do's" include correcting papers, attending meetings, preparing lessons, and talking to parents. The "want to do's" are teaching, working with kids, being creative, etc. Unfortunately, my personal "want to do's" don't have a high correlation with my "have to do's."

The other chapters in this book present time saving ideas in specific areas. This chapter might be considered a "catch-all" of twenty-five time savers which you might apply to your personal as well as your professional life. Not all of the ideas may be applicable to you, but you may find some that pique your interest.

⏰ Never be late

People who are late are either unorganized, egotistical, or suffer from the delusion that it is fashionable to be tardy. These are not professional attributes for which to strive. It is **not**

O.K. to be late to a professional obligation. Emergencies do occur, but they are rare. Get into the habit of being on time at all times.

What about doctors? barbers? repairmen? They're always late! What about my principal? He never starts on time and meetings go on and on! Yes, these are valid complaints. There's not much you can do about doctors, but you can work on your principal.

As a beginning teacher, I recall weekly staff meetings set to begin at 3:10. By the time everyone assembled it was closer to 3:20 and by the time anything of value happened it was 3:30. This was wrong and unprofessional. If it is happening to you, you need to work with your colleagues to change it.

Make an agreement with your staff and administration (make it part of negotiations, if necessary) that all meetings will begin on time as scheduled, have an agenda with the most important items appearing first, have an ending time which must be honored unless all participants agree to stay longer, and assure that no agenda item will appear more than twice without a decision being made. All participants must agree to be on time and do no other work (such as correcting) during the meeting.

If you can work toward this structure, you will find your meetings will be shorter, more professional, and less inclined to provide a forum for long-winded colleagues. You might even consider using five minutes per meeting to share ideas which are time savers. The ideal meeting should last no more than one hour. It is possible to enjoy staff meetings!

In terms of being on time in your classroom, have a set procedure to begin and end each teaching session (beginning of the day, after recess, etc.). Students need to be trained to be ready to work when the bell rings and *you* must be the role model. If you roll into your classroom thirty seconds late, guzzling a cup

116

of coffee while in a hurried/harried disarray, don't expect your students to behave any differently. If, on the other hand, you arrive early, have a consistent procedure, and appear in control from the opening minute, students will model this behavior as well.

As an aside, when you have appointments with doctors, hairdressers, et al., call before you leave and ask, "Is he/she on schedule?" One needn't be obnoxious about those who serve you being late, *but* there's nothing wrong with making it clear that you don't appreciate being forced to spend your time waiting for another professional.

Delegate completely and clearly

Much of what we do as teachers can be delegated to our students, paraprofessionals, parents, or classroom tutors. In the chapter, "Making the Grade," several ideas were presented on how to delegate your grading, but there are other areas in which you can delegate as well.

Most often overlooked are the tasks our students, individually, or as a group, can perform. Make a list of all of the tasks you have completed during the last several days. How many of these tasks could have been done by an aide, parent, or helpful student? Collating, duplicating, making charts, coloring overheads, typing a letter, collecting items to use in the room, etc. Five minutes of delegation to complete a twenty minute task is time well spent.

Two reminders -- when you delegate, you must do so completely, and therefore, run the risk of the outcome not matching your anticipated result. The times you will be disappointed will be heavily outweighed by the times your "delegatee" has gone above and beyond your expectations. Second, you must be very clear (especially with students) and anticipate all that can go wrong.

Effective delegation requires planning ahead. Most of the time, when we have to do something that could have been delegated, it is because we *didn't* plan far enough ahead. By the time we know *what* to delegate, it's too late to ask someone for their help!

⏱ Avoid keeping unnecessary records

This idea doesn't affect all who are reading this book, but there are undoubtedly many of you who are overdoing it with record keeping. Force yourself to use one simple system for keeping all of your pupil records and grades. Whether your district is using outcome based objectives, portfolio assessment, management by objectives, traditional grade books or any other record keeping system, use that system only. Don't keep double records.

If you are spending hours completing checklists each week (many teachers fit this description) either by personal choice or district requirements, either delegate the process or simplify your system. At most, you should have a grade book or register and one file folder per student. This should contain grades, sample work, discipline and observation information, correspondence with parents, and all other information on the student. A separate file folder for each of these items becomes an unnecessary burden.

The file folders which work best have twin prong fasteners at the top of the folder. These twin prong folders have a variety of formats, colors and dividers so student work can be kept by subject area. You will also need a two hole paper punch as well. These folders are very convenient for organizing and viewing student work at conferences as well as keeping work in chronological order.

🕐 Do the difficult or demanding things first

Studies indicate that seventy-five percent of your energy is gone by noon. If you have important mental tasks to perform, the best time to work on them is in the morning (not a great surprise to the average teacher). The time in the afternoon is best spent on short tasks that require less concentration. This means that you should probably do long range (creative) planning and organizing in the morning. Do your correcting and mundane tasks of preparing, duplicating, and collecting materials for the next day in the afternoon.

If you're going to spend time in the staff room, the later the better! Use your before school and recess time to organize and plan. Also, use the beginning of lunch period to prepare for the afternoon. When you've finished, eat lunch and relax.

🕐 Make decisions without "overanalyzing"

We make hundreds of decisions each day. The more quickly we make each decision and proceed on our way, the less time we spend worrying about the decision and the outcome. The worst that can ever happen is to be wrong and once you realize you've made the wrong decision, abandon it and make the right choice.

In most cases, if a decision is very difficult, *either* choice you make will have positive *and* negative side effect. There are usually several good solutions to a given problem so you may as well get started without overanalyzing.

$\textcircled{!}$ **Set time frames to "divide and conquer"**

When faced with a task which you don't want to do or which seems insurmountable for your mood, break it up into two or three small parts. For example, correcting sets of thirty essays might take two hours. Break this up into three, forty minute sessions. Set an alarm or timer for forty minutes (allowing for no interruptions for phone calls or visitors), correct like crazy until the alarm sounds and then walk away from the task to reward yourself with something you like to do.

Many people who set time frames are surprised how much they can accomplish in an uninterrupted block of time. Quite often, *things take the amount of time you let them take.* By dividing the task, it often becomes much shorter than imagined. In general, one hour of uninterrupted time (no phones, no contacts of any kind) is worth four hours of time with interruptions.

Buy an egg timer with a sixty minute countdown to set on your school desk and your work area at home. The slightly annoying grind of it ticking the moments away is a good reminder to stay on task. You'll soon learn to love the sound of its "ding" at the end of your allotted time because you'll know a reward is waiting.

$\textcircled{/}$ **Avoid over or under use of the telephone**

The telephone can be a boon or a nemesis to time management. It depends on how you use it. In terms of your profession, your phone conversations should be brief and to the point. The way in which you choose to use the phone in your personal life is not the issue here.

The ideal professional phone call lasts less than two minutes. It has a clear and specific purpose. If your professional calls to parents, students, peers last longer than two minutes, they have become personal calls in that you have begun to chat rather than deliver a message.

A two minute conversation is *very* brief, but if you have five calls to make each day, they will take at least ten minutes, even keeping the conversations to two minutes. There are techniques you can use to keep your calls brief and to the point.

Often we call parents who do not want the conversation to end. They like you, respect you, and want to talk to you. You need to preface your conversations with phrases such as: "I'm making a number of calls to parents this afternoon..." " I'm on my way out to a meeting in a moment, but I just wanted to alert you that..." "A colleague is waiting to meet with me, so I need to keep this very brief..." or, "I'd love to talk about this but I need to catch _____ before he/she leaves."

By opening the conversation and setting a time frame, you alert the listener that you have something important to say and that you're going to get right to the point. It puts the entire conversation into a different frame of reference. It also gives you the perfect excuse to hang up after your message has been delivered.

People will not think you rude for having brief conversations. When you receive a call from a professional or from their office personnel, they typically don't chat. They are busy and have many contacts to make each day. You too are a professional and should conduct phone conversations in the same way.

A second point to consider that whenever you call someone, you are interrupting them from another task. Most people would much prefer to be interrupted for two minutes rather than ten minutes. Two minute conversations can be every bit as friendly as longer conversations.

If you enjoy talking on the phone, as most people do, try to keep your personal and professional calls separate. If you are calling someone from school with whom you have a personal relationship and the subject is *business*, alert them with a introduction such as, "I'm wearing my teacher hat now and need to let you know that..." or "I'll call later to chat, but I need to let you know that..." Business and pleasure usually don't mix. Make your business calls from school and your personal calls from home.

There are a number of other aspects of phone use which, if put into practice, will make the phone a valuable ally in your teaching.

Keep a telephone log of all professional calls

Use a steno pad or notebook to log all your calls. Write the date, number, time of call, and a brief description of the subject of conversation. Don't write it on index cards or separate sheets of paper. Keep a log with wire bound pages so they will stay in chronological order. Be certain to write the date and time of each call and a brief description of the topic and result. If necessary, your phone notes can be transferred to your discipline/observation log (as described on page 78). This does create double record keeping, but it's much more convenient to have all calls to the same parent listed on one sheet when you do parent-teacher conferences.

This phone log is a legal document and will undoubtedly save you from embarrassing situations several times in your career. When you can show a parent or administrator *in writing* that calls were made at various times, and that discussions occurred on several occasions, you can feel rather smug (in some very volatile confrontations) that you have handled the situation professionally. Logging phone calls is a very important habit to develop.

Remember to log unanswered calls (including messages you leave on an answering machines).

Hang up on every sales call

I suppose there is some personal emotion in this suggestion because phone solicitation drives me crazy. Hanging up on anyone is difficult because it seems so rude; however, you owe a salesperson nothing, and he or she has intruded upon your time which is also rude. You can actually learn to smile as you say, "I'm not interested," as you hang up the receiver.

Pick your time to return calls

When you receive a phone message, it is not an emergency. When you receive an emergency call, you'll know it! Common courtesy dictates that calls should be returned, but return them at your convenience.

Calls to be returned to angry parents can be classified as "back burner" calls. A parent who is upset will probably not listen to you rationally. Place the call on the back burner and return the call the following day when the parent is at work. This accomplishes three objectives; first, the caller has had time to cool down and think about the situation, thus placing both of you in a better position for reasonable discussion; second, in a less hostile conversation it is more likely that neither of you will say something regrettable; third, surrounded by their work environment the parent is more apt to be subdued in discussing the concern.

Don't procrastinate when delivering bad news

Calls which you must initiate and dread making (discipline problems, failing grades, or contacting irrational parents, etc.) should be made as soon as possible. Procrastination only heightens your level of concern.

To look at this another way, it is far better to tell your side of the story to a parent *before* the student gets home and relates his or her version. This doesn't mean you won't hear back from the parent, but at least you have assumed the position of control by making the first contact.

Use the "callee's" answering machine to avoid return calls

When you are delivering a message or information to a parent and get an answering machine, leave your complete message on the machine. There's no point in asking them to return your call; a return call causes you to be interrupted while working on something else.

While on the topic of answering machines, *everyone but you* should have one! Answering machines make the caller's life easier. They shift the entire responsibility of completing a conversation to the other person. The owner of an answering machine must return calls, pay for them, get messages that are at times incoherent or are cut off by tape length, and have messages not record or be erased by another person. Anyone who really needs to talk to you will call back. If they call once and miss you and don't call back, the call probably wasn't very important in the first place. Don't buy an answering machine, but encourage those around you to do so.

Never argue on the phone (or anywhere else)

No one wins an argument so why participate? There is nothing wrong with *discussing*. "Agreeing to disagree" is a nice thought, but takes a sophisticated person on *both* ends of the phone line, and these days, this is becoming rare.

When talking on the phone and an argument begins, use one of the following responses to end the conversation: "You've caught me off guard with this information; let me take some time to think about what you're saying and I'll get back to you." "I have to check with the other parties involved, please give me some time to look into this and I'll get back to you." "Obviously we both feel strongly about this; let me take some time to see if I can work out a fair solution."

In other words, remove yourself from the situation and give the other person time to think about it. You'll usually find that the call back is much more pleasant for both of you.

If you anticipate a difficult phone call, begin with a statement such as, "We're in this together," or "How can we work together to help your son or daughter?" Realistically, both you and the parent want what is best for the child. Parents often need to be reminded that teachers and parents are on the same side and must work together.

Never lose control of your emotions

Regardless of what is said by the other person in a phone conversation, maintain your composure. A parent who uses profanity toward you or who is *off the wall* is probably used to strong confrontations. Don't fight it and don't accept it. End the conversation with, "I'll be happy to discuss this with you when you have calmed down," "I believe we've come to the end of this discussion (click)," or "I won't be threatened or talked to in this manner. If you're unhappy with me your next step is to talk to my principal." There is no reason that you should have to tolerate someone trying to badger or threaten you.

Document what was said and submit a copy to your administrator as soon as possible. You may also wish to send a copy of this documentation to the callers alerting them that you are keeping a record of your contacts with them. They won't like it but it does have a subtle message which people seem to understand these days.

Phone ahead before you leave for appointments

Many appointments or meetings can be handled by phone. A phone conversation is always shorter for all parties involved. If you must meet or if you have personal appointments with physicians, mechanics, or others, phone the person before you leave for the meeting.

You accomplish three things by phoning ahead. First, you assure that the appointment is firm and that your contact is on time. Second, you give your contact time to focus and prepare for *your* matter at hand before you arrive; this saves him or her from fumbling, searching, or being unable to answer your questions. You might even ask, "is everything ready?" when you make your call. This places all responsibility on your contact and gives him/her an out to reschedule if all is not complete. Third, it provides one last opportunity to handle the situation by phone before making a physical appearance.

The phone is your ally in time management. You can save between fifteen minutes and one hour per day by using the phone techniques described in this chapter.

⏲ Set office hours and make appointments

An open door policy (total availability to visitors) is a wonderful thought, but it can and usually does become uncontrollable. Your first obligation is to yourself, then to your students, and then to visitors. If you are too available to parents and fellow teachers before, during, and after school you can't possibly have enough time to plan, correct, and teach. You definitely won't have enough time to pursue your other interests away from school.

Be accessible but only at certain times. *You must set office hours and you must have visitors make appointments.* For example, your office hours might be from 7:30 - 8:00 every Monday and Wednesday morning and from 3:00 - 4:00 every Tuesday and Thursday afternoon. Let your school secretary know your schedule and have her direct parents to make appointments within these limits.

Don't allow yourself to meet with parents on a "drop in" basis. Of course you need to greet them each morning and exchange pleasantries, but don't conference during non-office hour times.

Attorneys, physicians, business people, and other professionals make appointments -- often well in advance -- *because their professional time is valuable.* Rest assured, as a teacher, your professional time is more full and far more regimented than most other professionals can even imagine. You only have so much time each day, so assume the stance of other professionals.

⊕ **Use turf**

This topic is an adjunct to the previous topic in that you must establish the setting for conferences and meetings. It refers not only to the location but also the posture and the tone of the meeting.

When you meet with a parent who insists on talking to you but has no appointment, don't invite them into the room to sit. Stand at the doorway or better yet in the hallway to conduct this discussion. There are levels of comfort in a discussion. Standing outside is the least personal and will often generate the shortest conference; sitting inside the classroom is very personal and will usually cause a longer discussion.

You can move a parent from inside the room to the outside with remarks such as, "I need to check on my students," or "I need to catch so and so when she goes by." These statements can be delivered with a sense of commitment to duty so that your visitor cannot question or take offense to your professional obligations.

Think about and plan different ways in which you can abbreviate or avoid unscheduled conferences and meetings. Of course, when you have a scheduled appointment, courtesy and common sense dictate that you should sit down and talk to your guest.

⊕ **Don't interrupt others**

Avoid being the cause of others' interruptions. Teaching is a social occupation and it's important that we talk, share, and commiserate with fellow teachers, but not to the point of dominating their free time. This is listed as a time saver only from a point of awareness that we can be a time waster to others.

⏱ Avoid blaming time

As mentioned in the introduction, twenty-four hours is all that any of us get each day. It's probably the most equitable resource that we have; yet, we have a tendency to blame time for going too fast or being in insufficient supply. If there is a culprit in this system, it's not time, it's your priorities in your use of time. You'll find that the more organized you become, the more time you'll have to do the things you want to do.

⏱ Reward yourself often!

What is the point of managing your time if all you do is work harder in the free time you have created? You must provide *tangible* rewards for your diligence and organization. The next chapter discusses goals and dreams, but in this case we're describing the small, day to day rewards that make your self-discipline worthwhile.

All rewards need not be a week's vacation or a cruise. Rewards can take many forms and might include such small pleasures as treating yourself to an ice cream cone, finding the time to write or call a friend, watching a football game, baking some cookies, going for a ride in your car or on your bicycle, buying something you've wanted, sleeping until noon, reading a book, going to a play, etc.

There are literally thousands of ways to reward yourself that range from a thirty second treat to a year-long vacation. Year-long vacations will probably have to wait, so reward yourself with something enjoyable, as often as possible.

The key is to *reward yourself with each completed project*. Unless you do this, you will find no comfort, enjoyment or satisfaction in time management. This is an essential component!

⏱ **Don't become upset about something over which you have no control**

There are very few of us who like to wait in line, sit in pointless meetings, get stuck in traffic, wait for people who are late, have a car break down, or stop for the construction crew that is repairing the road, but each one of these situations will occasionally happen to all of us.

There are two approaches you can take which can help you appreciate the moment. First, enjoy the fact that for at least a few minutes you have absolutely nothing to do! (It's really rather nice if you look at it with this perspective.) A second approach is to always carry something with you to occupy these moments. It might be a book or magazine, a cassette or CD player with headphones, a sketch book, your appointment book, writing paper and pen, a computer game, a newspaper, a crossword puzzle, or any other diversion you enjoy.

If you are prepared for these "wait times" and have something which you like to do, sit back and enjoy the wait!

⏱ **Accept less than perfection in you and in others**

At times in our lives we may get close to perfection. Most of the time, however, *very good* and *my best* are acceptable. A step down from this is, *at least it's finished,* and that is often all you really need. This is true for yourself and for those around you.

People who strive for perfection worry a lot and are rarely, if ever, satisfied. This doesn't mean that we shouldn't strive for the perfect solution or product; it simply means that after we've made a one hundred percent effort that involves planning and care, we must accept the result and move on.

Perhaps we learn from our mistakes and do better the next time; or the task takes less time in the future due to the practice we've had.

Don't be afraid to be less than perfect!

Avoid working hurriedly

A frantic pace is pointless. Even when deadlines are near, relax and move methodically through your project. If you can break the job into segments or tasks, do so, and give yourself time frames to complete each portion.

If you have a deadline, which, after analyzing the task, you know you cannot meet, let people know as soon as possible. Take the pressure off as quickly as you can, and you will find that the feeling of being *rushed* has vanished.

People who are always in a hurry make others nervous. Intensity and dedication towards a task are respected, but a person who frantically accomplishes tasks is not much fun to be around. You can avoid a hurried or rushed approach through thorough planning and by being honest about your limitations.

Have written goals

In effective time management, there is ***nothing*** more important than having written goals. Without making a commitment in writing, goals are nothing more than ideas.

131

Your written goals are the purpose for managing your time. Without goals, you have nothing measurable to accomplish. What's the point of managing your time if you don't have a plan for the time you've acquired?

If the word *goal* sounds too structured for you, substitute *priorities* or *dreams*. It doesn't matter what you call them as long as you identify them. For example, if some of your short term goals include having time to read a book each week, going to a cultural event, spending more time with your family, and going out to dinner once a week, write them down in a place where you'll see them every morning and throughout the day. They will give you a purpose or incentive to adopt many of the ideas presented here. Your goals become part of your reward for practicing time management.

Goals do not represent a "to do" list, they represent an *"I want to do"* list. Manage your time on your *to do's* and the *want to do's* will follow. But first, the *want to do's must be written down.*

This applies to your students as well. They must be taught and encouraged to set goals for themselves. After you have established your goals list, as described in the next chapter, work through this same process with your students. It seems a bit altruistic, but you will find that teaching goal setting to children can change their entire outlook towards school.

🕐 Use an organizer

The easiest way to avoid forgetting important items is to write things down as they are mentioned to you. With the amount of input you receive each day from teachers, parents, students, bulletins, and announcements, you can't possibly remember to do all that you are asked.

Find an organizer system which is small enough to be portable and carry it with you at all times. It's easiest if it will slip into a pocket or purse. In one small organizer you can keep your calendar, important phone numbers, to do lists, reminders, expenses and mileage (if necessary), and your all important list of goals.

Get in the habit of making a note while the person is talking to you; otherwise, you'll have another interruption and forget to jot it down.

⏱ Avoid most procrastination

Putting things off is a fault which most of us share. Our lives would certainly run more smoothly if we handled each challenge as it arose, but that is not human nature.

There are many books and articles written about procrastination in which the tone reflects the attitude that all procrastination is bad. A suggestion is that you adopt the philosophy to *avoid most procrastination*. Putting things off for a time can solve many problems. Time is a great healer and often allowing a day or two (at times a week or two) to pass before handling a task can be beneficial.

The two situations which should never be procrastinated: when you are truly worried about settling the issue at hand or when you damage your reputation by procrastinating.

If you have an unpleasant task to perform such as calling an uncooperative parent about their child's misbehavior, calling your insurance company about a recent accident, dealing with the Internal Revenue Service, talking to a colleague with whom you have a disagreement, or worrying if you have enough money in the bank to cover the check you wrote, don't procrastinate in completing these responsibilities. You gain nothing by waiting, and you put yourself through turmoil by worrying. Face the music and handle the situation.

What other people think of you as a professional is very important. The higher their regard for you, the less time you will spend explaining or defending your actions to them -- this includes parents, students, and peers. Avoid procrastinating in any situation which might damage your reputation.

If you have an obligation such as a presentation for a staff meeting, making phone calls to organize a conference, meeting a school deadline for grades or forms, or returning papers to students that have been promised by a certain time, don't procrastinate. People will view you as inefficient and unorganized.

When can procrastination be beneficial? When you have to return a call to an irate parent (page 123), when you are considering setting up a meeting of any kind (see next section), when you are angry at someone and want to confront them, when you are about to discipline a child out of anger, when you postpone a new task to first reward yourself for completing another obligation, when you wait for students to completely grasp a concept before charging ahead into the next unit. There are many more situations which you might identify.

There is an associated word which you might think of as a synonym for "procrastination." It has a much more positive connotation... *patience*. For some reason, most people view procrastination as a nemesis while considering patience as a virtue. They are really very similar!

The next time someone asks you to stop procrastinating, simply reply that you are being patient and that you're going to give the problem some time to resolve itself. It's all in how you look at it!

⊙ **Eliminate unncesessary meetings**

Have you ever met anyone who was upset that a meeting was cancelled? If you don't have much to say, or what you have to say can be postponed, cancel.

⊙ **Keep your desk neat**

The appearance of your desk makes an impression on every person who walks into your classroom. A desk is an extension of your personality. If you don't believe that, think about the desks of those you know.

This doesn't mean that a desk needs to be completely clear, but it needs to be (or at least appear to be) organized. Do you know everything you have in your desk? Can you put your hands on everything without searching? Do you have all of the things you need in your desk? Do you have only one desk?

If you answered "no" to any of these questions, reorganize and stay organized. Not only does your desk make an impression upon others, it makes a profound subconscious impression upon you. If you have stacks of materials, develop a filing system (see "Disciplining Your Management" chapter). If you have bits and pieces of things you haven't used in more than two or three years, throw them away. If you use your desk as the year long supply cabinet, find another place to store the extras and keep only what you need in the desk. If you have equipment (stapler, pencil sharpener, etc.) that only work half the time, get rid of them and get new ones.

How do your students manage their desks? Be an example to them of what a desk should be, and teach them to be professional students by taking pride in their organization.

⏰ Establish standard procedures

Many of the tasks, both professional and personal, that we perform each day are repetitive and mundane. Weekly and monthly obligations can also be repetitive. Since you have to perform these tasks so often, develop methods to complete the tasks efficiently and without thought. Most often, these routine procedures can be done by students, your children, or a parent volunteer.

One of the most beneficial procedures for teachers is a five minute planning session at lunch time or at the close of school. Take five minutes and write down all that needs to be done before you arrive at school the next morning. This includes marketing, going to the dry cleaners, picking up and dropping off kids, deciding on dinner and breakfast menus, renting a video, getting clothes ready, correcting papers, etc.

If you are a person who is rushing every morning to get organized, and if your entire life seems to be running a few minutes late, make an effort to establish standard operating procedures.

⏰ Have a plan for your extra time

You need to "plan" how you will spend your extra time. This doesn't mean you need a minute by minute description of how to spend your weekend, but you do need to "block" the time you plan to save for yourself and avoid, *with absolute resolve*, any attempt by others to fill this block of time with other obligations.

If you are incorporating the ideas in this book with the hope of having time to improve your golf game, then you must schedule or plan your golf time. Don't let any other obligations which might arise interfere with your plan.

Make an appointment for your tee off times as much in advance as possible. Lock them into your schedule and don't change them. This accomplishes two objectives. It ensures you'll get to do what you want to do most, and it gives you an opportunity to look forward to doing it! Anticipation is often half the fun of an activity.

If you don't plan your free time, unforeseen obligations will take the time away, and you'll rarely do the things you really want to do.

⊙ **Don't try to look busy**

People who appear busy usually spend much of their time *trying* to look busy. We all have many obligations and commitments. We each can do only one or two things at a time. Concentrate on the matter at hand in a relaxed manner. It's all that you're going to accomplish at that particular moment anyway. Rewarding yourself between tasks is the best way to feel "unbusy."

⊙ **Say "NO"**

Saying *no* takes practice, courage, and commitment. It's probably the most important word to use effectively *if* you want to have time for your priorities. Fortunately, there are techniques you can use which soften the effect of saying *no* to a friend or fellow teacher.

If you want to gain the time to accomplish the goals you have in mind, you cannot allow colleagues to place their responsibilities on you. The more you accept, the more they and others will ask you to do. There are times when you must accept extra work and extra responsibilities, but in general, if you learn to say *no* effectively, you will save hours and hours of time.

Rule 1

Don't say *yes* immediately. Either say *no* or "I need some time to think about it." When someone catches you off-guard with a request for your time, there is nothing wrong with putting off your response. Give yourself time to think about it. Weigh the positives and negatives and then get back to the person with your decision. If it fits into your priorities, accept; if it conflicts with those things you want and need to accomplish, decline.

Rule 2

Program yourself to say *no* and have pat answers to support your response. For example:

"No, I have several obligations that I need to complete and I just can't take on anything else."

"No, that is not really an area of interest to me and I don't think I'd do a real thorough job."

"No, I don't have the background in that area and I'd have to do a lot of research to know where to begin."

"No, I just made a commitment to myself to complete (some task) and I need to focus on that."

"No, but have you thought about asking ....."

"No, but in taking just a quick look, have you thought about doing it this way...?"

You needn't provide a long list of all you have to do or all of the things that are happening in your life. Simply say *no*, give a brief reason and go on to the next topic. Justifying your decision by talking too much is a sure sign of guilt.

Rule 3

If in doubt, say "no." You can always go back and say yes. The person who made the request will usually be pleased. The opposite is not true. Once you've said *yes*, you are generally stuck with your commitment.

Rule 4

If it's a situation in which you can't say *no*; say *yes* with a qualification such as:

"Well, O.K., but it will take me about five days until I can get to it."

"Yes, but you'll need to help me prioritize my other duties so you understand why other things aren't getting finished."

"Yes, I'll be happy to do this for you but in return will do .... for me?"

"Yes, I'll get to it right away, but may I work on it at home (may I have Friday off to get it done)?"

"Yes, but could this be considered an 'overtime' assignment with overtime pay?"

As you develop your list of priorities, it will become easier to say *no* to co-workers, your boss, and friends. You would certainly never want to alienate yourself from these people, but you also cannot live your life catering to other peoples' priorities. Knowing how to say *no* puts you in control.

Enjoy the moments

Everyday in your classroom, there are those wonderful moments of student innocence, brilliance, and humor. The same is true in your personal life. Enjoy those moments, even write down those things that made you smile or laugh. You are teaching because you want to give of yourself. Always take time to allow yourself to appreciate what children and young people have to share.

Making Time Work
for You

Those of you who have listened to a motivational speaker, know the excitement and exhilaration you feel immediately after the speech. With time, the enthusiasm fades and eventually you are left with a few ideas here and there which are put into practice but eventually forgotten.

This is not a "put down" of motivational speakers, they are inspiring and encouraging. However, human nature causes our enthusiasm to fade with time. I mention this because it is my hope that what you have read in this book will not fade, but become and integral part of your life.

I assume that you have read this book because you want to have more free time. The time to do the things which are a high priority in your life; in other words... *to achieve your goals*.

You may want to spend more time with your friends or family, have time to read, volunteer in a local program of some kind, work a second job, or finish your Master's or Doctorate. You may want to sleep longer on the weekends, watch more television, or just have time to sit and do nothing. Your goals may be noble or grandiose: to travel around the world, write the great American novel, become politically active, or learn to speak five languages. The possibilities are endless and there are no goals that are "wrong."

In time management books and seminars, goal setting is usually an important component. The speaker or author inevitably emphasizes that establishing priorities or setting goals is a natural adjunct to managing your time. Once you've established your goals, the experts also agree that the most important step in accomplishing a goal is to *write it down*. There is something compelling about making a commitment in writing.

It is not foolish to write that you want to sleep until 11:00 every Saturday and Sunday, or that you want to have time to sit and watch television each night with your family without feeling guilty. It is not silly to write that you want learn to speak French fluently, to make $100,000 per year, and to own your own home. If these are your priorities, then your free time should be spent enjoying or pursuing these activities.

If you don't write your goals and review them each day, you won't accomplish them! The extra time you've created, via time management, will become filled with other activities that are not your priorities.

How do you go about generating a list of goals? There are several techniques that I've used with fellow teachers and students which are described on the next few pages. The ideas tend to overlap, so while you won't do all of the activities, you might combine two or three of them to generate your set of goals.

Stream of consciousness writing

Set a timer or an alarm for twenty minutes and find a place where you won't be interrupted by kids, phones, or extraneous sounds. Using a pen or pencil (use one which *feels* good as you write) and a pad of paper, write nonstop until the alarm sounds. Write about what you've done in your life, what you care about, what you want to do, about your dreams, about your perfect day, etc. Don't worry about spelling, punctuation, sentence structure, or capitalization.

You may find that twenty minutes is not enough time. If so, keep writing after the bell rings, but as a minimum, spend at least twenty minutes writing.

Do this stream of consciousness writing three or four times over the next week or two and you'll find that certain topics or ideas keep appearing. From these writings, generate a list of *"ten goals I'd like to accomplish with my free time"* and put them into a heirarchy, item one being the most important, and item ten being least important.

You will probably have some very broad topics listed. These may need to be divided into a workable format such as the grid or time line as described on pages 141 and 142.

What I can do well, what I can't do well, and what I want to do well

Divide a sheet of paper into three columns. Use the headings given above as column titles. Over a span of two or three days, keep adding to this list. Remember, these are your own thoughts, so you do not need to share them with anyone. The information is yours and yours alone.

Don't be shy about bragging, being truthful, or dreaming. We all have attributes, habits, idiosyncracies, hobbies, wishes, and dreams that fit each of these column headings. You need to write your ideas regardless of how silly, unattainable, or self-serving they might seem. Dreams and goals aren't necessarily practical in their "raw" state.

Once you have completed your categorized list, you need to look through each column and make some decisions.

Your first column, "What I can do well" should have many entries. If you have not listed at least ten of your attributes here, take time and write them. If you feel there aren't ten good things to write about yourself, you have one to add immediately -- "I am not egotistical!"

Once you have ten items listed, look through the list and circle three activities which, even though you can do well, you want to improve upon. Label them: 1, 2 and 3 (first, second and third priority).

The second column, "What I can't do well" should have at least five entries. Since you've identified these "weaknesses," it's probably an indication that you'd like to improve in at least some of these areas. Circle three that you'd like to work on, and prioritize them: first, second, and third.

The third column, "What I want to do well," may have overlapping topics from columns one and two. Cross out any of the duplicate items from the first two columns. From those remaining, circle three that you most want to accomplish and prioritize them.

You have identified nine goals to work on. Do some soul searching, and decide if you really want to attain the nine goals you've listed. If so, make a commitment that you are going to complete one activity, pertaining to each goal, every week.

For example, imagine that two of your goals are: to take five salary units per year and to arrive home from school at 4:00 each day. This week, find a class in which to enroll, and put one suggestion from this book into operation. At the end of the week, you won't have five units or be home by 4:00, but you will have taken a measurable step in achieving your goals.

Complete one step towards each goal, each week, and you'll be amazed how quickly you will accomplish your nine objectives.

Categorize your dreams

Make a grid and label it as shown, below. If you did the stream of consciousness writing, this grid is a good way to organize your random thoughts. If you are using this activity as a means of generating your goals, you need to spend at least a week carrying this grid with you and looking at it every time you have a *break* in your day. Different locations and situations spark new thoughts and ideas.

	Short Term Goals 1 month - 1 year	Middle Term Goals 1 year - 5 years	Long Term Goals 5 years - 20 years
Professional			
Family			
Personal			
Health			
Financial			
General			

Develop a time line

Some of your goals can be accomplished in a very short period of time. Some are contingent upon the completion of others. Some will not be realized until the distant future. With this in mind, you may find it helpful to put goals into a time frame.

The time frame might also be viewed as a *plan of action*. Once you've identified five or ten major goals, break them down into monthly or quarterly parts or pieces. Changing a dream into reality can take many steps. For example, if one of your goals is to buy a house in five years, there is certain information you need to gather to make it happen.

1. Save $25,000 for a down payment
2. Learn about the real estate market
3. Learn about loans, points, closing costs, interest, etc.
4. Decide where you want to live
5. Learn how much you need to earn to qualify for a loan
6. Learn about the tax advantages of owning
7. Get to know some real estate agents
8. Learn about schools and communities
9. Learn something about quality of construction

Once you have a list of what you need to know, develop a timeline to keep yourself moving towards completion.

	Year 1	Year 2	Year 3	Year 4	Year 5
Save $25,000	Save $3,500	Save $4,000	Save $4,500	Save $5,000	Save $5,500
Real Estate Market?					
Points or Interest?					
Where to live?					
Loan Qualify					
Tax savings					
Real Estate Agents					
Schools/Community					
Construction					

While this may look somewhat daunting, it brings your goal into perspective. If saving $3,500 seems impossible, maybe you will need to motivate yourself to take ten units each year to increase your pay. Perhaps the $200,000 home you dream of is out of the question from the start; if so, you need to re-evaluate where you will live, or lower your expectation of the type of house you can afford.

Perhaps a financial advisor can help you develop a tax-sheltered annuity plan to save money for your down payment. Maybe a real estate agent can find a creative financing plan, such as a lease purchase or owner financing, to enable you to purchase the home you want.

Sometimes the dream isn't easy and at times the obstacles may seem overwhelming, but the point is, *if you don't plan, and if you don't follow your plan, **nothing** will happen!*

● ● ●

Regardless of how you establish your goals or what goals you establish, they mean nothing unless you make a commitment to accomplish them. I hope that by implementing some of the ideas presented in this book, you will have the time to broaden your outlook and to have more time for... you.

If you take nothing else from my suggestions, other than realizing that *you have the ability to be in charge of your time,* I still feel positive about what I have shared.

The days of the little red school house have long since passed. The demands put upon teachers are greater than ever before. It's time that issues such time management, the professional workplace, managerial skills, and self-fulfillment are adopted by all educators.

Education is the largest industry in the world, and we (teachers) are the CEO's and leaders of this industry. We need to make it our business to operate our industry successfully, efficiently, and professionally. All it takes is time.